Nicholson's

WATERWAYS GUIDE
2 MIDLANDS

The waterways covered by this book are

Ashby Canal Marston Junction to Snarestone
River Avon Tewkesbury to Stratford-upon-Avon
Birmingham Canal Navigations navigable sections of the BCN
Birmingham Canal Main Line Gas Street Basin to Aldersley Junction
Stourbridge Canal Stourton Junction to Delph, including the Stourbridge Arm
Birmingham & Fazeley Canal Farmer's Bridge Junction to Fazeley Junction
Coventry Canal Coventry to Fazeley and Fradley Junctions
Grand Union Canal Bugbrooke to Leicester and Birmingham
Oxford Canal Banbury to Hawkesbury Junction
River Severn Tewkesbury to Bewdley
River Soar (Grand Union Canal) Leicester to the River Trent
Staffordshire & Worcestershire Canal Stourport to Great Haywood Junction
Stratford-on-Avon Canal King's Norton Junction to Stratford-upon-Avon
Trent & Mersey Canal Derwent Mouth to Stone
Worcester & Birmingham Canal Worcester to Birmingham

Other books in this series are

1 South   **3** North

ROBERT NICHOLSON PUBLICATIONS

A Nicholson Guide

First published 1978
Second revised edition 1981

© **Robert Nicholson Publications Limited 1981**

Based on the original research and observations
of Andrew Darwin and Paul Atterbury

Maps based upon the Ordnance Survey with the
sanction of the controller of Her Majesty's
Stationery Office. Crown copyright reserved.

Robert Nicholson Publications Limited
24 Highbury Crescent
London N5 1RX

Printed in England by E. T. Heron, Silver End
Witham, Essex

ISBN 0 905522 47 8

*Front cover: Atherstone Locks on the Coventry
Canal. Derek Pratt.*

Introduction

The waterways of England and Wales have emerged from a long period of decline into an exciting period of restoration. All over the network, disused canal arms and basins are being dredged, new marinas are being built and whole lengths of canal once left to decay, are now pleasant cruiseways. In urban areas, the 'muddy ditch' at the back of the factory is being turned into a 'linear park' for the whole community to enjoy. Credit for this new lease of life must go in turn to the many societies whose members work during their spare time campaigning, clearing and rebuilding, to those enlightened local councils who are recognising the amenity value of the waterways, and of course to the British Waterways Board.

Built originally as efficient trade routes, the network today provides a unique retreat from a noisy and impersonal world, where boaters, walkers, fishermen, those interested in natural history or industrial archaeology can peacefully enjoy the beauty and quiet isolation of these once busy waterways. There is interest for everyone in the canals: the engineering feats like aqueducts, tunnels and flights of locks; the brightly decorated narrowboats; the wealth of birds, animals and plants on the canal banks; the mellow architecture of canalside buildings like pubs, stables, lock cottages and warehouses.

This series of three guides covers not only BWB waterways, but also some navigable rivers such as the Thames and the Avon, and the privately owned Bridgewater Canal. These form essential links in popular circular cruising routes.

The maps show all necessary navigational information—bridges, locks, tunnels, junctions—and the text describes the route and services available. Boatyards are listed and indicated on the maps and there is a selection of pubs and restaurants. We hope these books will guide you successfully on your journeys as well as provide you with an insight into a very valuable part of our national heritage.

Contents

Symbols

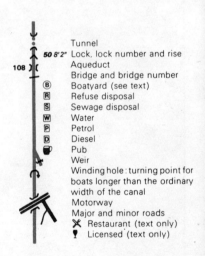

Tunnel
50 8'2" Lock, lock number and rise
108 Aqueduct
Bridge and bridge number
Ⓑ Boatyard (see text)
Ⓡ Refuse disposal
Ⓢ Sewage disposal
Ⓦ Water
Ⓟ Petrol
Ⓓ Diesel
☕ Pub
Weir
Winding hole: turning point for boats longer than the ordinary width of the canal
Motorway
Major and minor roads
✗ Restaurant (text only)
🍸 Licensed (text only)

The Country Code
Guard against fire risks
Fasten all gates
Keep dogs under proper control
Keep to paths across farm land
Avoid damaging fences, hedges and walls
Leave no litter
Safeguard water supplies
Protect wildlife, wild plants and trees
Go carefully on country roads
Respect the life of the countryside

The maps are ½ inch to 1 mile scale

The distance given under the name of the section is the approximate mileage on that particular page

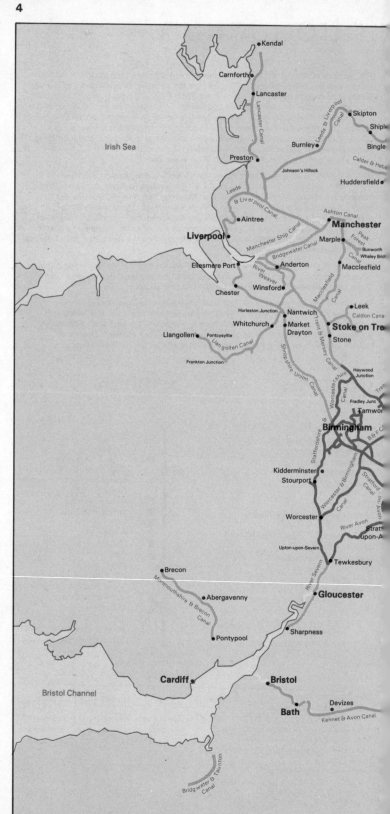

Kendal

Carnforth

Lancaster

Lancaster Canal

Leeds & Liverpool Canal

Skipton

Shiple

Bingle

Burnley

Irish Sea

Preston

Johnson's Hillock

Calder & Hebe

Huddersfield

Leeds & Liverpool Canal

Ashton Canal

Manchester

Peak Forest

Aintree

Liverpool

Marple

Buxworth

Whaley Brid

Manchester Ship Canal

Bridgewater Canal

Macclesfield

Ellesmere Port

Anderton

River Weaver

Winsford

Macclesfield Canal

Leek

Caldon Cana

Chester

Hurleston Junction

Nantwich

Whitchurch

Market Drayton

Stoke on Tre

Llangollen

Pontcysyllte

Stone

Llangollen Canal

Trent & Mersey Canal

Frankton Junction

Shropshire Union Canal

Haywood Junction

Tren

Worcestershire Canal

Fradley Junc

Tamwor

Staffordshire & Worcester Canal

Birmingham

B & F C

Kidderminster

Stourport

Stratford on Avon Canal

Worcester & Birmingham Canal

Worcester

River Avon

Strat upon-A

Upton-upon-Severn

Tewkesbury

Brecon

River Severn

Gloucester

Monmouthshire & Brecon Canal

Abergavenny

Sharpness

Pontypool

Cardiff

Bristol

Bristol Channel

Bath

Devizes

Kennet & Avon Canal

Bridgwater & Taunton Canal

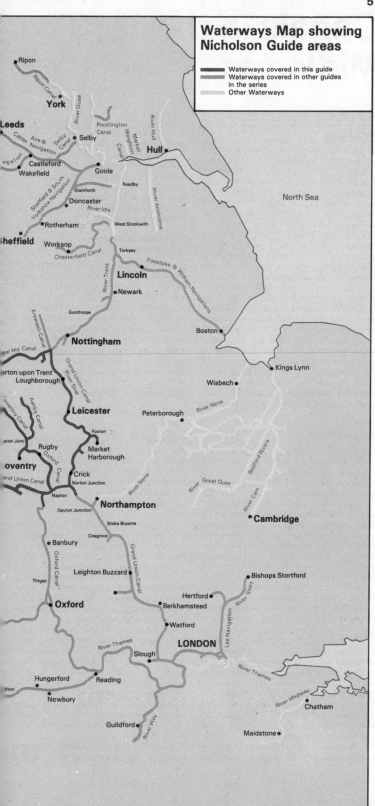

Waterways Map showing Nicholson Guide areas

Waterways covered in this guide
Waterways covered in other guides in the series
Other Waterways

Ripon
Ripon Canal
York
River Ouse
Leeds
Aire & Calder Navigation
vigation
Castleford
Wakefield
Selby
Selby Canal
Pocklington Canal
Market Weighton Canal
River Hull
Hull
North Sea
Goole
Keadby
River Ancholme
Stainforth
Sheffield & South Yorkshire Navigation
Doncaster
River Idle
heffield
Rotherham
West Stockwith
Worksop
Chesterfield Canal
Torksey
River Trent
Lincoln
Fossdyke & Witham Navigations
Newark
Gunthorpe
Boston
Erewash Canal
rsey Canal
Nottingham
Kings Lynn
rton upon Trent
Loughborough
Grand Union Canal
River Soar
Wisbech
River Nene
Peterborough
oventry Canal
Leicester
Foxton
ton Junc
Rugby
Oxford Canal
Market Harborough
River Nene
Bedford Rivers
Anthy Canal
oventry
nd Union Canal
Crick
Norton Junction
Napton
Gayton Junction
Northampton
River Great Ouse
River Cam
Cambridge
Banbury
Stoke Bruerne
Cosgrove
Oxford Canal
Grand Union Canal
Bishops Stortford
Thrypp
Leighton Buzzard
Hertford
Berkhamstead
River Stort
Oxford
Watford
LONDON
Lee Navigation
River Thames
Slough
River Thames
Hungerford
Reading
ton
Newbury
River Medway
Chatham
Guildford
River Wey
Maidstone

Canals in the Midlands

Background

Since before mediaeval times, when the Severn was one of the main trade highways of England, there has been a continuous history of inland navigation in—or rather to and from—the Midlands. In the 17th century some of the earliest attempts to improve navigation by the construction of locks were carried out on the rivers Avon, Trent, Stour and Salwarpe, though not all were wholly successful. One of the most enthusiastic and far-sighted promoters of transport by inland waterways at this time was Andrew Yarranton, a Worcestershire man. The remains of the primitive 'flash-locks' which he built around 1653 on the little Dick Brook to serve his iron furnace and forge at Shrawley may still be traced. Despite the growing industrial development of the Midlands, the seed sown by Yarranton did not immediately germinate, and it was over a century before any further progress was made. In the meantime initiative had passed to the north, where the first modern artificial waterway, independent of a natural water course, was the Bridgewater Canal, opened in 1759.

James Brindley

The engineer for this pioneering project was James Brindley, a Derbyshire millwright of ingenuity and vision. Sponsored by the ambitious young Duke of Bridgewater and supported by his resourceful agent John Gilbert, Brindley built in Lancashire a canal that excited the curiosity of the world. In the 14 years between his first involvement with inland waterways and his death, at the age of 56, in 1772, he attracted the title of 'The Father of English Canals', a title which might easily have been Yarranton's had he lived in more propitious times. Brindley's success on the Bridgewater Canal assured his reputation, and he naturally became heavily involved in other canal projects. He surveyed and superintended construction of the Trent and Mersey Canal, authorised in 1766, and reckoned by Brindley to be the first stage of the 'Grand Trunk Canal', his vision of a waterway system stretching from coast to coast, east to west and north to south. The Staffs and Worcs Canal, authorised in the same year, provided an outlet from the Midlands to the river Severn; and the Coventry and Oxford Canals of 1768 and 1769 respectively completed a link to the Thames and thus to south-east England. Brindley died with only the Staffs and Worcs line finished; but his great projects continued, and did much to encourage industrial growth in the Midlands and stimulate the construction of further canals. Ultimately the Midlands had the most intricate network of waterway connections anywhere in Britain, and even today when that network has contracted, it provides an unequalled wealth of interest for the industrial archaeologist.

Early canal development in the Midlands

The Midland canals vary enormously in character, and this is related to the topography of the land over which they pass, and also to their period of construction and the engineering skills of the time. When Brindley began on the Staffs and Worcs, the first Midland canal completed, he had no accumulated fund of experience on which to draw. As a pioneer, he was carefully feeling his way with a series of experimental features, leaving as little as possible to chance. His attitude gave this canal perhaps the most distinctive character of all.

The Staffordshire and Worcestershire Canal

Brindley's first aim was to reduce engineering works to a minimum. This he achieved by following the gentle valleys of the rivers Penk, Smestow and Stour. It was almost certainly this intention from the outset that led him to create a new canal port, Stourport, at the confluence of the Stour and Severn.

Where engineering works were unavoidable, Brindley played safe on every possible occasion. His early locks on the Staffs and Worcs, for example, had chambers which leaned outwards: it was thought that their 'battered' sides would be better able to resist lateral thrust due to frost action or clay movement; and even now his locks are less liable to damage during severe winters than the later vertical-sided ones.

His aqueducts display similar caution. The biggest and most characteristic spans the Trent at Great Haywood, only yards from the junction with the Trent and Mersey. Almost an embankment with a series of large culverts rather than a true aqueduct, its massive proportions carry not only the water but also a tremendous weight of earth and puddled clay bed, and only three low stone arches admit the flow of the river below.

Heavy lockage was avoided in several places by rock cuttings and by a couple of short tunnels at Cookley (65 yards) and Dunsley (25 yards); but at one point, the Bratch in Wombourn, Brindley encountered a sudden drop which could not be avoided by these means. He overcame the problem by building three locks, each with its own set of upper and lower gates, so close together that only four feet separated the top gates of the lower locks from the bottom gates of the ones above. The level of the intermediate lock was maintained through culverts running from side-ponds. This arrangement is unique, and one can imagine Brindley looking at what he had built and coming to the conclusion that considerable economies in masonry and timber, as well as easier working, could be achieved by using the bottom gate of one lock as the top gate of the next, in 'staircase' pattern. When he came to another sharp drop less than two miles away at Botterham, he built a double lock to this new design.

The side weirs to the locks on the Staffs and Worcs are particularly interesting. Brindley designed an ingenious experimental circular weir, with the sill taking the form of a shallow saucer, the culvert entrance being a vertical hole in the centre, the effect being that of an enormous funnel. These weirs occupy far less space than a straight weir of equal capacity, and are also less liable to jamming, as debris collects in the saucer, from which it can be readily removed. Examples may be seen at Stewponey, Awebridge and Wightwick Mill locks. It was found, however, that the increased cost of construction greatly outweighed the advantages of these weirs, and they were not used on any other canal.

Many bridges over the Staffs and Worcs Canal still retain their original oval cast-iron plates giving their names and numbers in bold lettering. Individual bridges of particular merit include number 46 (Bumble Hole Bridge), and number 109 at Great Haywood Junction. The most influential bridge design on the Staffs and Worcs, however, was a type of footbridge used on the southern section. It was of cast iron and had a cantilever form, with a division in the middle to allow the passage of the towrope, a device later adopted on the Stratford-on-Avon Canal. None of the originals are now usable by towing horses, but several examples remain, e.g. at Falling Sands Lock near Kidderminster.

Other Brindley canals

Brindley's caution on his engineering works and his attempts to follow the contour principle, which often created an extremely beautiful, sinuous and lengthy course—but which was much cheaper to construct and maintain—are both reflected in other early Midland canals. His Birmingham Canal (1768–72) had the first long lock flight in the Midlands—20 (later increased to 21) at Wolverhampton—but its true character is better represented by the exaggerated meanderings of what are now (since Telford straightened out the canal) the Wednesbury Oak Loop, Oldbury Loop, Cape Loop, Soho Branch, Icknield Port or Rotton Park Loop and Oozells Street Loop. These were later superseded as through routes by Telford's alterations and not all are now passable. Brindley's Oxford Canal (1769–90) has also been drastically straightened north of Napton Junction, but parts of the original line survive as the Wyken Colliery Loop, Stretton Wharf Arm, Fennis Field Limeworks Branch, Newbold Arm, Barby Loop and others. His Coventry Canal (1768–90) and Stourbridge Canal (1776–9) have been little altered. The last major contour undertaking was the western section of the Wyrley and Essington Canal (1792–5), which has particularly notorious bends at Sneyd Junction and the 'Devil's Elbow' in Wednesfield.

'Second generation' canals, 1780–1820

With increasing experience, canal engineers became more ambitious, and the next generation of canals, constructed in the two decades either side of 1800, witnessed some phenomenal efforts, with canals being taken straight across increasingly difficult terrain by means of more elaborate engineering works. John Smeaton (builder of the Eddystone Lighthouse) was among the first to adopt the new approach on his Birmingham and Fazeley Canal (1784–9), which has an unusually high number of lock flights over its 20-mile course: 13 at Farmer's Bridge in Birmingham, 11 at Aston, 3 at Minworth and 11 at Curdworth, with a further 6 at Ashted on the Digbeth Branch (1799). There is also a short tunnel at Curdworth.

The Worcester and Birmingham Canal

The most interesting product of this phase is the Worcester and Birmingham Canal, authorised in 1791 to provide Birmingham with a more direct route to the Severn. This proved to be one of the most arduous and costly (£610,000) canals yet built. Apart from considerable natural obstacles, the unfortunate proprietors suffered continual embarrassment by costly disputes over water rights and exorbitant compensation demands, and it was not finally completed until 1815. It shared with the Trent and Mersey the distinction of possessing the greatest number of tunnels on any single canal line: from the north. Edgbaston (105 yards), King's Norton (2726 yards), Shortwood (608 yards), Tardebigge (568 yards) and Dunhampstead (236 yards). It was originally intended as a barge canal, so all the tunnels were built wide. Tardebigge Tunnel caused construction problems, being cut mostly through solid rock with only a small portion brick-lined. King's Norton is curious in that the north portal is quite pretentious, in strong contrast to the unadorned south portal. Edgbaston Tunnel was the only one provided with a towpath, but Dunhampstead was worked by means of handrails fixed to the wall. In the other tunnels, tugs were later used to pull the boats through.

This canal involves heavy lockage: in the 16-mile rise from the Severn at Worcester there are no fewer than 58 locks. Apart from three separate flights of six each at Offerton, Astwood and Stoke Prior, this includes the Tardebigge Flight, which with 30 narrow locks in two miles is the biggest in Britain.

In Tardebigge Top Lock it also has the deepest narrow lock in England, with a fall of 14 feet. The explanation here is that it replaced an experimental vertical lift, the first example known, designed by John Woodhouse in 1809. This lift consisted of a single wooden tank balanced by metal counterweights. But the cost of construction and maintenance of the lift proved prohibitive, and for the remainder of the descent locks were employed, the prototype lift itself being replaced by a single deep lock soon afterwards.

The Stratford-on-Avon Canal

Financial problems also bedevilled the Stratford-on-Avon Canal, construction of which began in 1793 from a junction with the Worcestershire and Birmingham Canal at King's Norton. By 1796 construction had reached Hockley Heath, but most of the authorised capital was spent, and a temporary terminus was made there. In 1799 work resumed and the canal was taken as far as Lapworth where, following a deviation from the route originally planned, a branch was built with one lock leading down to the Warwick and Birmingham Canal (now part of the Grand Union) at Kingswood Junction, completed in 1802. Shortage of funds again halted the project here until 1812 when the final stage to Stratford was commenced. It was completed in 1816 to the Bancroft Basins in Stratford, with a link to the Avon not originally intended and authorised only the previous year.

The only tunnel on the Stratford-on-Avon Canal is at Brandwood near King's Norton: 352 yards long, it was built to a 16-foot width, sufficient for two boats to pass within; fixed handrails were provided for haulage. Its west portal is ornamented with a circular plaque bearing Shakespeare's portrait and a laurel spray, and flanked by two niches; the east portal also has niches and an inscription (now illegible). Much of the canal is heavily locked, with 55 locks in only 15 miles: the main groups are at Lapworth (25) and Wilmcote (11). But the chief engineering feature of the Stratford-on-Avon Canal is its aqueducts. There is a large brick one over the river Cole on the canal's northern section, but the three most interesting ones are all on the southern section. In strong contrast to Brindley's aqueducts these are relatively lightly built, the water being contained in iron troughs. The biggest is the Bearley or Edstone Aqueduct, built by William Whitmore: 475 feet long, it crosses a road, a stream and two railways; its tow-

ing-path is slung beside the waterway like that on the first iron-trough aqueduct built in England, at Longdon-on-Tern on the Shrewsbury Canal. Wootton Wawen Aqueduct is of similar construction and date, supported on girders and brick pillars. The third and smallest, at Yarningale Lock, was added in 1834 after the original was washed away in a flood. It is a tiny aqueduct, taking the canal over the river Alne.

The Dudley Canal

The Dudley Canal is noteworthy for possessing three of the longest canal tunnels in the Midlands. The earlier was the Dudley Tunnel. Lord Dudley and Ward had begun a private canal about 1775 from the Birmingham Canal through a short tunnel to the Tipton Colliery workings, later extended with the building of the subterranean Castle Mill Basin to serve the extensive limestone quarries. In 1785 the Dudley Canal Company began to extend their original modest line by five locks at Park Head (or Parkhead) and then in 1792 through a great 2,942-yard tunnel to join Lord Dudley's tunnel at Castle Mill Basin, whence a further 196 yards of the old tunnel led back into the open. This gave a total length from end to end of 3,154 yards. Between 1805 and 1837 Lord Dudley built a further underground branch from Castle Mill Basin for some 1,277 yards to serve the limestone workings of the Wren's Nest. The specified dimensions of the Dudley Tunnel were: width 9 feet 3 inches, depth of water 5 feet 6 inches, and headroom 7 feet. Passage was by legging throughout, and much of the length is through solid rock. Strenuous efforts to restore this remarkable underground waterway system resulted in its re-opening to navigation in 1973, along with the formerly impassable Parkhead locks. The same, alas, cannot be said for the even longer Lappal Tunnel (3,795 yards) on the Selly Oak Extension (or No. 2 line) of the Dudley Canal, built 1796–7. Part of it, affected by mining subsidence, collapsed in 1917 and was abandoned. Today nothing remains visible of this, the third longest canal tunnel in Britain. A third tunnel, Gosty Hill, remains on that part of the Dudley No. 2 line which is still navigable: 577 yards long, it has one solitary ventilator. There are two places within where the roof drops alarmingly in height. The fourth important tunnel is Netherton (see below).

The Warwick canals

Two further canals of this phase are the Warwick and Birmingham (authorised 1793) and Warwick and Napton (1794), both completed in 1800, both absorbed into the Grand Union system in 1929, and together opening a shorter route from Birmingham to London. There are several lock flights: 21 at Hatton, 9 at Stockton, 6 at Knowle (later reduced to 5), 6 at Camp Hill, 4 at Bascote and 3 at Calcutt. Of the several aqueducts, the most impressive carries the Warwick and Napton on three stone arches over the river Avon at Emscote. But the engineers for these two canals were less able than some of their fellows, and the Blythe Aqueduct collapsed soon after its building in 1795. One tunnel of 433 yards was built at Shrewley, but owing to a shortage of funds modifications had to be made to the original line to avoid further tunnels at Yardley, Rowington and Leamington. Another modification for the sake of economy was to join the Oxford Canal at Napton instead of crossing it at Braunston as had originally been intended.

Telford and the 'third generation' canals

The third phase of canal-building marked the peak of the canal engineers' achievement, but also coincided with increasing railway competition. The name of Thomas Telford is outstanding in this period (as was that of Brindley in the pioneering stages). Telford first appears on the scene in 1824 when the Birmingham Canal Navigations, or BCN—an amalgamation of the earlier Birmingham, Birmingham and Fazeley and Wyrley and Essington Companies—commissioned him to survey their outdated and overloaded Birmingham—Wolverhampton main line. This had remained virtually unimproved since its construction except for the replacement of Brindley's wasteful 491-foot Smethwick Summit in 1787 by a new summit built by Smeaton on the 473-foot 'Wolverhampton' level. The top three locks of Brindley's flights of six at Spon Lane and Smethwick had then been abandoned, and three new locks added parallel to the surviving Smethwick three to supplement them.

Telford's modernisation of the BCN

Telford's recommendations were executed between 1825 and 1838. A new feeder reservoir at Rotton Park and the straightening of the line between Birmingham and Smethwick came first. Then a completely new line was begun from the bottom of Spon Lane locks, parallel to Brindley's cut, but on the 453-foot 'Birmingham' level rather than the 473-foot level, via Dudley Port, rising to rejoin the old line by three new locks at Tipton. At the end of 1829 Telford made the great cutting, 70 feet deep, through the hill at Smethwick on the 453-foot level: the three parallel summits of Brindley, Smeaton and Telford at different levels on the same slope are a unique feature here.

Telford's Smethwick cutting was spanned by the great Galton Bridge, a single iron span of 150 feet, cast at the Horseley Ironworks in Staffordshire. It was then the largest canal bridge in the world; it has now been closed to traffic for its own protection, while beside it two brand-new canal tunnels have been constructed. (Comprehensive road-building required that the canal cut-

tings on the Birmingham and Wolverhampton level should both be covered over for a distance of about 100 yards each, leaving room for spacious canal tunnels with new roads on top.) Other notable structures of the BCN include the Stewart Aqueduct, carrying the Brindley line across the Birmingham Level to the top of Smeaton's reduced flight of Spon Lane locks, and the superb cast-iron Telford aqueduct which carries the Engine Arm from Smeaton's 473-foot level over the 453-foot level. This branch, built 1789–90, took its name from the first Boulton & Watt steam engine bought by the canal company to pump water up to the Smethwick summits; the engine itself is now in retirement at the Birmingham Museum of Science and Industry. A third aqueduct, the Ryland Aqueduct, carried Telford's line over the Dudley Port Road. But this was replaced by a new concrete structure in 1968 to allow the road below to be widened.

The last major re-alignment of the Birmingham Canal main line was completed in 1837 and cut off the Wednesbury Oak Loop between Bloomfield and Deepfields junctions by a broad tunnel 360 yards long, with twin towpaths, through Coseley Hill. In 1836 the Gower Branch provided a further link between the Birmingham and Wolverhampton levels by the three Brades locks, the top two of which formed the only staircase formation in the entire BCN.

By 1839 the whole line from Birmingham west to Aldersley Junction (where it met the Staffs and Worcs Canal) had been improved to the new standard, 40 feet wide, with twin towpaths throughout. Twin-arched bridges such as that below Tipton Factory locks are characteristic of the 'new' canal, as is a dead straight course running alternately through deep cuttings such as Smethwick, and on high embankments, such as that east of Dudley Port.

Oxford Canal improvements

Similar straightening operations took place on other canals. The Oxford Canal Company was forced to improve its competitive position by straightening out its route north of Braunston, so during 1829–34 Telford was commissioned to execute a series of short cuts, amounting virtually to a new waterway which drastically shortened Brindley's original circuitous route. A 250-yard tunnel with twin towpaths replaced the old Newbold Tunnel; the old loop and tunnel at Wolfhampcote were replaced by an embankment, entailing a change of site for Braunston Junction (the original junction was the entrance to the present boatyard). Brinklow Aqueduct was widened and made into an embankment; and a new iron aqueduct was built near Brownsover. Where the old loops were retained for the sake of their village wharves the new towpath crossed over via graceful Horseley Ironworks bridges, contrasting with the older brick bridges.

Further improvement of the BCN

In 1836 the Lodge Farm Loop of the Dudley Canal was by-passed by the new 75-yard Brewin's Tunnel, which was opened out into a cutting some years later; other loops at Dudley Wood and Bumble Hole were similarly cut off. Elsewhere, completely new canals were still being built around this time. The Birmingham and Warwick Junction Canal (now part of the Grand Union system) was opened in 1840, linking the Warwick and Birmingham to the Birmingham and Fazeley Canal. It is so straight that seven successive road bridges can be seen in line under the arch of the first; the five Garrison locks and Nechells Shallow Lock bring it to the level of the Birmingham and Fazeley Canal at Salford Junction. Almost opposite is the entrance to the Tame Valley Canal, opened the same year; this is even more modern, being deep and wide, with twin towpaths, long straight stretches and alternate embankments and cuttings. Both were built to avoid bottlenecks: the former bypassed the Ashted and Aston flights, saving 17 locks; the latter route, via the 13 Perry Barr locks, provided an alternative to the desperately congested Farmer's Bridge Flight. The Rushall Canal (1847) is similar with its long pound below the second Rushall Lock running dead straight for over a mile. So too were the Bentley Canal (1843) and (outside Birmingham) the Droitwich Junction Canal (1853), both now derelict.

Netherton Tunnel

Amongst the greatest engineering feats of this period was the Netherton Tunnel, built by the BCN company in 1855–8 as a bypass to the narrow and usually congested Dudley Tunnel. The last canal tunnel built in England (with the exception of the two rather different tunnels now completed—as mentioned above), Netherton was also the most sophisticated. Like Coseley and Newbold tunnels, it was given twin towpaths throughout and was wide enough to allow two-way working—indeed, with a width of 27 feet at water level (of which each towpath occupied 5 feet), a centre water depth of 6 feet, and a headroom of nearly 16 feet, it had the largest bore of any English canal tunnel. It was well ventilated, with

seven airshafts. Moreover, it had a lighting system, worked first by gas, later by electricity; the remains of the turbine which produced the power are still to be found just outside the northern portal. A greater contrast with Brindley's rough rock-cut short tunnels or the claustrophobic Lappal or old Dudley Tunnels could hardly be imagined.

The Cannock Extension

The last important canal built in the Midlands was the Cannock Extension, opened between 1858 and 1863 to connect the BCN with the developing Cannock Chase coalfield. Its straightness and blue brick bridges are typical of the railway age. It is now closed off beyond Norton Canes, mining subsidence having destroyed most of the rest, including the Churchbridge locks linking it with the Hatherton Branch of the Staffs and Worcs Canal.

The Grand Union Canal modernisation scheme

One final important development on the Midland canals before nationalisation in 1947 was the absorption of the three Warwick canals in 1929 by the new Grand Union Canal Company. This company embarked on a government-backed programme of improvement in the 1930's, including bank reinforcement and piling (much of it is marked with the date), and the widening of the canal to take 14-foot barges. All the old narrow locks between Calcutt Bottom Lock and the top of the Camp Hill Flight were converted to weirs, and may still be seen alongside the new broad locks. On the Knowle Flight six locks were replaced by five; and at Bascote two separate locks were replaced by a staircase pair. Near 'The Boatman' pub at Braunston may still be seen the entrance to the basin formerly used for transhipment from barges to the narrowboats working on the northern Oxford Canal. All the lock paddles on the new locks were built with an enclosed housing, which makes them easier to operate and less dangerous. By this time, however, the heyday of commercial traffic on the canals had passed, and the improvements failed to produce the hoped-for increase in trade and revenue.

Cruising information

Licences

Pleasure craft using BWB canals must be licensed and those using BWB rivers must be registered under the British Waterways Act 1971. Charges are based on the length of the boat and a canal craft licence covers all the navigable waterways under the Board's control. Permits for permanent mooring on the canals are also issued by the Board. Apply in each case to:

Craft Licensing Office,
Willow Grange,
Church Road,
Watford WD1 3QA.
(Watford 26422).

The Licensing office will also supply a list of all BWB rivers and canals. Other river navigation authorities relevant to this book are mentioned where appropriate.

Getting Afloat

There is no better way of finding out the joys of canals than by getting afloat. The best thing is to hire a boat for a week or a fortnight from one of the boatyards on the canals. (Each boatyard has an entry in the text, and most of them offer hire cruisers; brochures may be easily obtained from such boatyards.)

General Cruising

Most canals are saucer shaped in section and so are deepest in the middle. However very few have more than 3-4ft of water and many have much less. Try to keep to the middle of the channel except on bends, where the deepest water is on the *outside* of the bend. When you meet another boat, the rule of the road is to keep to the right; slow down, and aim to miss the approaching boat by a couple of yards; do not steer right over to the bank unless the channel is particularly narrow or badly overgrown, or you will most likely run aground. The deeper the draught of the boat, the more important it is to keep in the middle of the deep water, and so this must be considered when passing other boats. If you meet a loaded working boat, keep right out of the way. Working boats should always be given precedence, for their time is money. If you meet a boat being towed from the bank, pass it on the outside rather than intercept the towing line. When overtaking, keep the other boat on your starboard, or right, side.

Speed

There is a general speed limit of 4mph on most British Waterways Board canals. This is not just an arbitrary limit; there is no need to go any faster, and in many cases it is impossible to cruise even at this speed. Canals were not built for motor boats, and so the banks are easily damaged by excessive wash and turbulence. Erosion of the banks makes the canal more shallow, which in turn makes running aground a more frequent occurrence. So keep to the limits and try not to aggravate the situation. It is easy to see when a boat is creating excessive turbulence by looking at the wash. If in doubt, slow down.

Slow down also when passing moored craft, engineering works and anglers.

Slow down when there is a lot of floating rubbish on the water; old planks and plastic bags may mean underwater obstacles that can damage a boat or its propeller if hit hard.

Slow down when approaching blind corners, narrow bridges and junctions.

Running aground

The effective end of commercial traffic on the narrow canals has meant a general reduction in standards of dredging. Canals are now shallower than ever, and contain more rubbish than ever. Running aground is a common event, but is rarely serious, as the canal bed is usually soft. If you run aground, try first of all to pull the boat off by reversing the engine. If this fails, use the boat hook as a lever against the bank or some solid object, in combination with a tow rope being pulled from the bank. Do not keep revving the engine in reverse if it is obviously having no effect; this will merely damage both your propeller and the canal bed by drawing water away from the boat. Another way is to get your crew to rock the boat from side to side while using the boat hook or tow rope. If all else fails, lighten your load; make all the crew leave the boat except the helmsman, and then it will often float off quite easily.

Remember that if you run aground once, it is likely to happen again as it indicates a particularly shallow stretch – or you are out of the channel:

In a town it is common to run aground on sunken rubbish, for example old oil drums, bicycle frames, bedsteads etc; this is most likely to occur near bridges and housing estates. Use the same methods, but be very careful as these hard objects can easily damage your boat or propellor.

Remember that winding holes are often silted up do not go further in than you have to.

Mooring

All boats carry metal stakes and a mallet. These are used for mooring when there are no rings or bollards in sight, which is

How a lock works

Plan: lock filling

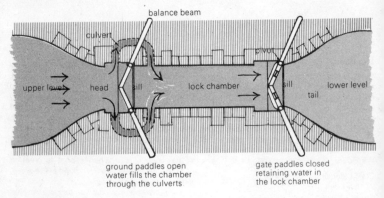

balance beam

culvert

pivot

upper level

head | sill | lock chamber | sill | lower level

tail

ground paddles open
water fills the chamber
through the culverts

gate paddles closed
retaining water in
the lock chamber

Elevation: lock emptying

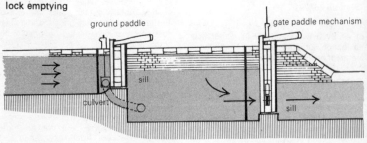

ground paddle

gate paddle mechanism

sill

culvert

sill

ground paddles closed
preventing water from
the upper level filling
the chamber

gate paddles open
water flows from the
chamber to the
lower level

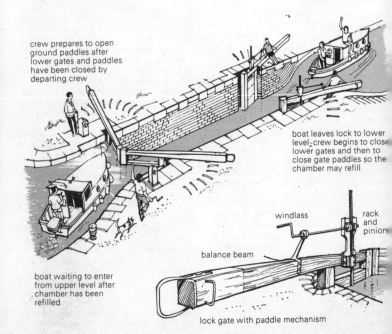

crew prepares to open
ground paddles after
lower gates and paddles
have been closed by
departing crew

boat leaves lock to lower
level; crew begins to close
lower gates and then to
close gate paddles so the
chamber may refill

boat waiting to enter
from upper level after
chamber has been
refilled

windlass

rack
and
pinion

balance beam

lock gate with paddle mechanism

usually the case. Generally speaking you may moor anywhere to BWB property but there are certain basic rules. Avoid mooring anywhere that could cause an obstruction to other boats; do not moor on a bend or a narrow stretch, do not moor abreast boats already moored. Never moor in a lock, and do not be tempted to tie up in a tunnel or under a bridge if it is raining. Pick a stretch where there is a reasonable depth of water at the bank, otherwise the boat may bump and scrape the canal bed—an unpleasant sensation if you are trying to sleep. For reasons of peace and quiet and privacy it is best to avoid main roads and railway lines.

Never stretch your mooring lines across the towpath; you may trip someone up and face a claim for damages.

There is no need to show a riding light at night, except on major rivers and busy commercial canals.

So long as you are sensible and keep to the rules, mooring can be a pleasant gesture of individuality.

Locks

A lock is a simple device, relying for its operation on gravity, water pressure and manpower.

On the opposite page, the plan (top) shows how the gates point uphill, the water pressure forcing them together. Water is flooding into the lock through the underground culverts that are operated by the ground paddles: when the lock is full, the 'top' gates (on the left in the drawing) can be opened. One may imagine a boat entering, the crew closing the gates and paddles after it.

In the elevation, the bottom paddles have been raised—opened—so the lock empties. A boat would of course float down with the water. When the lock is 'empty', the bottom gates can be opened and the descending boat can leave the lock.
Remember that:

1. For reasons of safety and water conservation, all gates and paddles must always be left closed when you leave a lock.

2. When going *up* a lock, a boat should be tied up to prevent it being thrown about by the rush of incoming water; but when going *down* a lock, a boat should never be tied up, or it will be left high and dry.

3. Windlasses should *not* be left slotted on the paddle spindle. If the ratchet slips (and they are often worn) the spindle will spin round and the windlass will fly off, probably into the lock or into someone's face.

4. Be very careful when operating locks in wet weather: the lockside is often slippery and the wooden planks across the gates can be downright treacherous.

Knots

You do not need to know much about knots is there is one that is generally useful, the clove hitch. This is simple, strong, and can be slipped on and off easily. Make two loops in a rope, and pass the right hand one over the left; then drop the whole thing over

a bollard, post or stake and pull it tight. See diagram below.

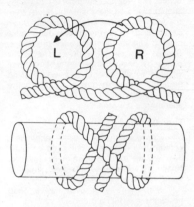

When leaving a mooring coil all the ropes up again. They will then be out of the way, but ready if needed in a hurry. Many a sailor has fallen overboard after tripping on an uncoiled rope.

Fixed bridges

At most bridges the canal becomes very narrow, a means of saving building costs developed by the engineers. As a result careful navigation is called for if you are to avoid hitting either the bridge sides with the hull or the arch with the cabin top. As when entering a lock, the best way to tackle 'bridgeholes' is to slow down well in advance and aim to go straight through, keeping a steady course. Adjustments should be kept to a minimum for it is easy to start the boat zig-zagging, which will inevitably end in a collision. One technique is to gauge the width of the approaching bridgehole relative to the width of the boat, and then watch one side only, aiming to miss that side by a small margin—say 6in; the smaller you can make the margin, the less chance you have of hitting the other side of the bridge. If you do hit the bridge sides when going slowly it is not likely to do much damage; it will merely strengthen your resolve to do better next time.

Swing bridges

Swing bridges are an attractive feature of some canals; they cannot be ignored as they often rest only 2 or 3ft above the water. Generally they are moved by being swivelled horizontally, or raised vertically. Operation is usually manual, although some have gearing to ease the movement. There are one or two mechanized swing bridges; these are very rare, and they have clear instructions at control points. Before operating any swing bridge make sure that any road traffic approaching is aware of your intention to open the bridge. Use protective barriers if there are any and remember to close the bridge again after you.

Swivel bridges, which are moved horizontally, are usually simple to operate. They do however demand considerable strength, and many are difficult for one person.

Lift bridges, which are moved vertically, are raised by pulling down a balance beam. The heaviest member of the crew should swing on the chain that hangs from the beam. Once the bridge is up the beam should be sat on or otherwise held as in some cases it fails to counterbalance the bridge. Serious damage could be caused to the boat and to the helmsman if the bridge were allowed to fall while the boat was passing through. A draw bridge is another, more traditional type of lift bridge; the method of operation is the same.

Tunnels

Many people consider a canal incomplete without one or two tunnels, and certainly they are an exciting feature of any trip. Nearly all are easy to navigate, although there are a few basic rules:

Make sure your boat has a good headlight in working order.

If you can see another boat in the tunnel coming towards you, it is best to wait until it is out before entering yourself. It is in fact possible for craft of 7ft beam to pass in many tunnels, but it can be unnerving to meet another boat. If you do, keep to the right as usual.

In most tunnels the roof drips constantly, especially under ventilation shafts. Put on a raincoat and some form of hat before going in.

A notice on the tunnel portal will give its length, in yards, and will say whether unpowered craft are permitted to use it.

Care of the engine

Canal boats are powered by one of three types of engine; diesel, petrol and petrol/oil or two-stroke. However basic rules apply to all three. Every day before starting off, you should:

Check the oil level in the engine.

Check the fuel level in the tank.

If your engine is water-cooled, check that the filter near the intake is clean and weedfree. Otherwise the engine will overheat which could cause serious damage.

Check the level of distilled water in the battery, and ensure that it is charging correctly.

Lubricate any parts of the engine, gearbox or steering that need daily attention.

Check that the propeller is free of weeds, wire, plastic bags and any other rubbish. Although this is an unpleasant task, it is a constant necessity and will remain so as long as canals continue to be used as public rubbish dumps. The propeller and the water filter should be checked whenever there is any suspicion of obstruction or overheating—which may mean several times a day.

When navigating in shallow water, keep in mind the exposed position of the propeller. If you hit any underwater obstruction put the engine into neutral immediately. When running over any large floating object put the engine into neutral and wait for the object to appear astern before re-engaging the drive.

Great respect should be shown to the engine. Remember that this simple main-

tenance could make the difference between trouble-free cruising and tiresome breakdowns.

Fuel

Petrol engines and petrol/oil outboards are catered for by some boatyards and all roadside fuel stations. Fuel stations on roads near the canal are shown in the guide, and these should be considered when planning your day's cruise. Running out is inconvenient; remember you may have to walk several miles carrying a heavy can.

Diesel powered boats pose more of a problem in obtaining fuel, although their range is generally greater than that of petrol powered craft. Most boatyards sell marine diesel, which is tax-free and therefore very much cheaper (the heavy tax on fuels is aimed only at road vehicles). The tax-free diesel, which contains a tell-tale pink dye to prevent it being used in road vehicles, can only be sold by boatyards, which are still few and far between on the canals. BWB yards may let you have enough to reach the next boatyard. Some, but by no means all roadside fuel stations sell diesel, but at the higher price. A further complication is that diesel engines must not be allowed to run out of fuel, as their fuel system will need professional attention before they can run again. So route planning is very much more important for owners of diesel powered craft. The simple rule about fuel is—think ahead. It is advisable to carry a spare can.

Water

Fresh water taps occur irregularly along the canals, usually at boatyards, BWB depots, or by lock cottages. These are marked on the maps in the guide. Ensure that there is a long water hose on the boat (BWB taps have a $\frac{1}{2}$-inch slip on hose connection).

Lavatories

Some canal boats are fitted with chemical lavatories which have to be emptied from time to time. Never empty them over the side or just tip them into the bushes. Either empty them at the sewage disposal points marked on the maps, or dig deep holes with the spade provided. Boats with pump-out toilets must use the pump-out stations — usually boatyards and indicated in the text. Some BWB depots and boat yards have lavatories for boat crews.

Litter

Some canals are in a poor state today because they have long been misused as unofficial dumps for rubbish, especially in towns. Out of sight is only out of mind until some object is tangled round your propeller. So keep all rubbish until you can dispose of it at a refuse disposal point. (See the maps)

Byelaws

Although no one needs a 'driving licence' to navigate a boat on the waterways, boat users should remember that they incur certain responsibilities and duties, e.g. knowledge of correct sound signals. Prospective navigators are advised to obtain a copy of the byelaws relevant to the waterways on which they are to travel.

Navigation, touring circuits & distances

A fully co-ordinated network, the canals of the Midlands are not a radial system focused on a well-defined centre, but form a complicated pattern of interlinking trunk routes and branches, a pattern which at first seems random and formless, but which on close inspection turns out to be an accurate reflection of the growth centres and primary trade routes of the Industrial Revolution.

All this is good news for the canal boater today, for he is offered an enormous variety of cruising circuits of all sizes. Some of these circuits take a couple of hours to complete, others take a couple of weeks. Few are free of locks, most offer a balance of rural and industrial scenery, and all have their special features.

Planning a cruise

It is wise when planning a cruise to establish a means of calculating the time it takes to travel any given length of canal. This ensures that you can reliably arrange to meet friends further along the canal at or about a given time—or you can work out whether you will reach a shop or pub before closing time. And of course for those who have hired their boat for a week, it is vital to return on time to the starting point.

The time taken to navigate any canal depends, of course, on the average cruising speed of your boat and the amount of time it takes to negotiate the locks along the way. Both of these vary according to circumstances: for example the optimum cruising speed of a boat depends not only upon the type and size of the boat and its engine, but also the cross-section of the waterway, the amount of wash caused by the hull, and many other factors (bear in mind that a shallow or narrow waterway restricts the speed of any boat). And you must also remember that there is in any case an overall legal speed limit of 4 mph on all the Midland canals. In practice, 3 mph is a realistic canal cruising speed for most boats in the Midlands.

To the uninitiated, 3 mph may sound an unbearably slow rate of progress through the countryside; but a few hours of gentle cruising on a fine day is usually enough to convert most people to this pace. For only by proceeding at walking pace can you appreciate the peace and beauty of the countryside, watch the bird life, and see the scurry of voles, water rats and others as they suddenly notice the slowly approaching boat.

The length of time taken to work through a lock depends on several things: whether the lock is full or empty, wide or narrow, deep or shallow. It depends on the number and size of the paddles that control the sluices, on the presence or otherwise of other boats near the lock, and of course on the number and competence of the boat crew. Most people take around 10 minutes on average to work through a typical lock—or, to put it another way, they take as long to get through a lock as they would have taken to travel another $\frac{1}{2}$ mile. Herein lies the basis for a simple method of estimating time required to travel along a given length of canal: take the number of miles to be travelled and add half the number of locks to be negotiated on the way. This gives the number of 'lock-miles'. Divide this by your average cruising speed, and the result is the approximate length of time it will take, in hours. Thus if you intend to travel 30 miles, and there are 42 locks along the way, the calculation is as follows: 30 + (42 divided by 2) = 30 + 21 = 51 lock-miles. 51 divided by 3 = 17 hours. So this particular journey will take you around 17 hours, assuming your average cruising speed to be 3 mph and assuming you take about 10 minutes to get through the average lock. (If you're a beginner, it might take a little longer than this to start with.)

The lock-mile system is a crude but effective and extremely useful means of working out times taken on canal cruises. To refine the system, simply tailor it more closely to the actual cruising speed of your boat and the efficiency of your lock-operating technique. To fit the lock-mile system to the Midland waterways is not difficult, and it helps to show what a wide choice these canals offer in terms of one-week or two-week holidays. An excellent fortnight's trip, for example, would be the circuit formed by the river Soar and the Coventry, Oxford, Grand Union (Leicester Section) and Trent and Mersey canals. This is 170 miles and 74 locks long, and takes you through some of the very best parts of Leicestershire. You will see the Foxton locks, Braunston Tunnel and the delightful village of Shardlow. You will on this circuit also enjoy one of the longest level pounds in the country; and if you have time to spare you can explore the lock-free Ashby Canal (22 miles long—2 days there and back) or the meandering course of the unspoilt Market Harborough Arm, 5 miles long.

A good round trip in terms of contrasts would be the Grand Union main line, north Oxford, Coventry and Birmingham & Fazeley canals, which at 106 miles and 88 locks would be a reasonably energetic week's cruising. On this route you could see Braunston and Hillmorton, the long level of the north Oxford canal broken by the 11 locks at Atherstone, and then the industrial outpost of Fazeley. In Birmingham, you could either slip southwards along the Grand Union or have a quick foray into the nether regions of the Birmingham Canal Navigations. Once out in Warwickshire, you encounter the five wide but modern locks at Knowle (built in the 1930's). A few miles further on, the 21 locks of the Hatton Flight will impede your progress considerably; but if you try hard you might get through them in 1½ hours. Then you are in the valley of the Warwickshire Avon, and after passing Warwick and Leamington Spa you start locking up out of the valley again to rejoin the Oxford Canal at Napton.

The most enjoyable week-long cruising route of all is now complete. This is the circle formed by the Stratford-upon-Avon and Worcester and Birmingham canals and the rivers Avon and Severn. It is a 100-mile route of great beauty, taking in the lush fruit-growing area of the Vale of Evesham, the idyllic Stratford-upon-Avon Canal, the handsome but heavily locked Worcester and Birmingham Canal with its great tunnel at King's Norton, and the sweeping reaches of the river Severn. Towns on this circle include such historic places as Tewkesbury, Stratford and Worcester, which are all of enormous interest to the visitor and the countryside that separates them is green, rich and unspoilt. This circuit of waterways has been broken for over 100 years, because much of the river Avon has been unnavigable for that time, but the Upper Avon Navigation restoration scheme, which has been financed and executed almost entirely by volunteers, is now finished at last.

These three are but a small fraction of the potential number of circular cruising routes in the Midlands. A glance at a map will show the very large number of permutations possible just using these routes as a basis; but the best thing is to make up your own mind. Use the map to work out the number of miles and locks on the various routes, and refer to the individual canal maps to find out where you would like to go and what you would like to see. Relate this information to the amount of time you have available, and you should be able to come up with a few alternative plans. But never make the mistake of undertaking a longer journey than you really want. After all, there is no point in making your holiday a race against time, and even if your party does not want to do much stopping to explore places near the canal, you will still *have* to stop here and there to buy food. So when planning a trip, always leave yourself plenty of time spare. Many a canal holiday has been spoilt by over-ambitious planning.

Watford Locks

Ashby Canal

The Ashby Canal was originally planned as part of a possible broad canal route from the Thames, via the Grand Junction, Oxford and Coventry Canals to join the River Trent at Burton. It was finally built to provide an outlet to the south for the coalfields near Ashby-de-la-Zouch, and was never extended north of Moira.

Completed in 1802, its first 20 years were unprofitable, but it eventually became successful as the demand for good quality coal from Moira increased. It was purchased in 1845 by the Midland Railway who continued the commercial transport of coal along the canal up to the turn of the century. Even today, the occasional narrow-boat carries coal from Gopsall Wharf.

Subsidence from coal mines near Measham caused the abandonment of the last nine miles, the canal now ending just north of Snarestone. With no locks and wide bridges the canal is ideal for quiet, relaxed cruising through little known and unspoilt country.

The Ashby Canal Association produce a map and guide which can be obtained from a box at Snarestone Junction (BWB key) or the Ashby Narrow Boat Co. A certificate can be claimed by those who navigate to Snarestone.

Maximum dimensions
Length: 72'
Beam: 7'
Headroom: 6' 6"
MARSTON JUNCTION (Coventry Canal)
to
Burton Hastings: 3 miles
Hinckley Wharf: 6 miles
Stoke Golding Wharf: 8¾ miles
Dadlington: 10 miles
Shenton Aqueduct: 13 miles
Market Bosworth Wharf: 15 miles
Congerstone: 17¼ miles
Shackerstone: 18¼ miles
Snarestone Tunnel: 21 miles
CANAL TERMINUS: 21¾ miles
There are no locks on the Ashby Canal

12½ miles

Leaving the Coventry Canal at Marston Junction, the scenery changes dramatically industry and housing are left behind to be replaced by green fields, farms, clear water and the wide stone arched bridges typical of this canal. This rural feeling continues as the canal passes Hinckley, where there is a short arm and follows the contour past Dadlington. Even the power lines that cross this area accentuate its remoteness from the other world to the west.

Burton Hastings
Warwicks. Pop 190. PO, tel, stores.
Quiet village in open farmland. Its pretty church has a font of 1300.
Hinckley
Leics. Pop 44,530. EC Thur. MD Mon.
All services. A manufacturing town where the first stocking machine in Leicestershire was installed in 1640. A row of timber framed cottages survive in Bond Street.
Higham on the Hill
Warwicks. PO, tel, stores. Quiet village on a hill overlooking the canal. The Motor Industry Research Association proving ground can be seen to the west.
Stoke Golding
Leics. EC Wed. PO, tel, stores, garage. The church is very beautiful, full of original 13thC and 14thC work. It is large, on a hill, and the spire dominates the landscape. Crown Hill, near the wharf, marks the place where Henry Tudor was crowned king after the battle of Bosworth Field in 1485.
Dadlington
Leics. PO box, tel. Village built around a green with much new development. The church dates from the 13thC.

BOATYARDS & BWB
Ⓑ **The Narrow Boat Company** The Canal Wharf, Stoke Golding, Nuneaton, Warwicks. (Hinckley 212671) Ⓡ Ⓢ Ⓦ Ⓓ Pump-out, hire cruisers, gas, moorings, toilets. *Open daily.*

PUBS
🏴 **Navigation** Marston Jabbett, near bridge 5. Food. *(Tel and garage nearby).*
🏴 **Lime Kilns Inn** Watling st, Hinckley. Canalside. Ⓡ Ⓦ
🏴 **George & Dragon** Stoke Golding.
🏴 **Dog & Hedgehog** Dadlington. Food.

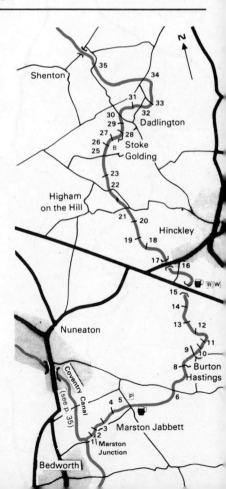

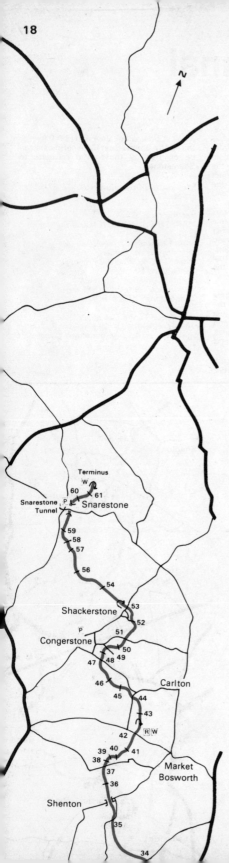

Market Bosworth

9¼ miles

The canal passes Shenton Park on an embankment, then on through light woods towards Congerstone and Shackerstone leaving Market Bosworth to the east. After Gopsall Park (where Handel is reputed to have composed the Messiah) the hills become more prominent. The canal passes under Snarestone through the only tunnel on the canal. Shortly after this the terminus is reached where there is a slipway, BWB sanitary station and picnic area. Subsidence has made it impossible to maintain the last nine miles to Moira. The setting is quiet, remote and wholly rural, with no hint of the industry that prompted the creation of the canal.

Shenton
Leics. PO box, tel. stores. Well-preserved estate village clustered around the Hall, a house of 1629 much rebuilt in 19thC. The Victorian church has a good 17thC monument. A large amount of home produce is offered for sale in the village.

Market Bosworth
Leics. Pop 1500. EC & MD Wed. PO, tel. stores, garage. Small market town remaining much as it was in the 18thC. The size and style of the church reflect the town's former importance. The Hall was extensively altered in the late 19thC.

Carlton
Leics. PO, tel. stores, garage. Small pre-industrial village.

Shackerstone
Leics. Pop 710. PO, tel. stores. Undeveloped and unchanged. Shackerstone is a farming village that reflects the pre-industrial feeling of the whole of the Ashby Canal. West of the village the canal flanks Gopsall Park; nearby is Twycross Zoo Park, well worth the walk from the canal.

Shackerstone Railway Society
The former Shackerstone Junction Station (near bridge 82), is coming to life again as a small railway museum and depot for steam locomotives. The Society has a ½ mile stretch of track and hopes eventually to extend to Market Bosworth. Enquiries to: Mr Tingay, Station House, Shackerstone (Tamworth 880408). *Open summer weekends.*

Snarestone
Leics. Pop 329. PO, tel. stores, garage. An 18thC farming village built over the top of the canal tunnel (250 yards). The Victorian Gothic waterworks, ½m N, mark the end of the canal.

BOAT TRIPS

Ashby Canal Association Narrowboat trips from Snarestone and Stoke Golding. Details from Hinckley 37226 (or 212178 evenings).

PUBS
🍺 **Red Lion** Park street, Market Bosworth. A good local.
🍺 **Gate** Carlton. Food.
🍺 **Horse & Jockey** Congerstone. Food.
🍺 **Globe Inn** Snarestone. Food.
🍺 **Rising Sun** Shackerstone. Food.

River Avon

Rising at Welford on the Leicestershire and Northamptonshire boundary, and joining the Severn at Tewkesbury, the River Avon has carried traffic since the 17thC. By 1665 the river was navigable to Stratford, and almost to Warwick by the early 18thC. In 1717 the navigation was divided into Upper and Lower sections, and in 1863, after several changes of ownership, the Upper section was sold to the Great Western Railway. By refusing tolls they were not obliged to do maintenance, and traffic on the section ceased in 1875. Dereliction was also setting in on the Lower section, and by the end of the 1939-45 war, navigation was not possible above Pershore. However, in 1949 determined efforts to restore the Lower navigation, led by Douglas Barwell, were successful. By 1964 Evesham could be reached by boat. Attention was now focused on the Upper Avon, and a team of voluntary labourers led by David Hutchings, MBE, worked continuously from 1969, dredging, clearing, and completely rebuilding locks and weirs. In June 1974 the Upper Avon New Navigation was officially opened by Queen Elizabeth, the Queen Mother, thus restoring a 110 mile circuit of splendid cruising waterways.

Maximum dimensions
Length : 70'
Beam : 13'6"
Draught : 3'6"
Headroom : 10'
Mileage
AVON LOCK TEWKESBURY to
Pershore Lock : 15¼
Evesham Lock : 26
Alveston Sluice Stratford : 46
Total 17 locks
See page 20 for navigational information.

---

13 miles

The River Avon joins the Severn less than ½m below Mythe Bridge, Tewkesbury. The passage between the Severn and Avon Lock has shallows which should be carefully avoided, and boats should keep close to the Town Quay beside the Mill. There are moorings on the right bank just below Avon Lock, convenient for the town. The river leaves Tewkesbury, passing under King John's Bridge, and enters a fine, wide stretch which is spanned by the M5 just before Bredon. The old Mill House at Strensham Lock has been reconditioned and has a resident lock-keeper who can supply tinned and frozen foods. There is also a water point. Access to Eckington village is easy from here, and requests for short duration mooring should be made to the lock-keeper. The village can also be reached from Eckington Bridge which has moorings to the right only. Mooring to the left bank is very dangerous. Birlingham village is a short walk from Birlingham Wharf which has overnight moorings. At Nafford Lock the swing bridge must be closed before leaving the lock. Nafford Island is a bird sanctuary and strictly private. Comberton Quay has overnight mooring and is convenient for Great Comberton.

Tewkesbury
Glos. Pop 8750. EC Thur, MD Wed, Sat.
This historic town was the site of a Yorkist victory in the Wars of the Roses in 1471. It has many timbered houses and some 13th and 14thC inns, including the Royal Hop Pole Inn, mentioned in 'The Pickwick Papers'. The impressive Abbey has a fine 132ft Norman tower.
Twyning Green
Worcs. Stores, PO. A short distance up the lane beside the Twyning Fleet Inn.
Bredon
Worcs. Stores, PO. Large, attractive village with some timbered houses, and a fine 14thC Tithe Barn owned by the National Trust, *open daily.*
Bredon Hill 3m NE of Bredon. 961ft high. There is a castellated Gothic folly on the slopes and the remains of prehistoric and Roman earthworks at the summit. Excellent views.

Eckington
Worcs. Stores, PO, station. The church dates
from the 12thC. Eckington Bridge, built
in the 16thC, is still in good condition.
Woollas Hall (Eckington 308). Elizabethan
Manor House containing fine paintings and
furniture. Viewing by appointment.

Great Comberton
Worcs. Stores. A path from the village leads
up Bredon Hill. About 2m E of the village is
Elmley Castle with its half-timbered cottages
and church of St Mary which contains fine
medieval sculpture.

BOATYARDS & FACILITIES

Ⓑ **Tewkesbury Marine Services**
St Mary's lane. (Tewkesbury 292187).
Ⓡ Ⓢ Ⓦ Ⓓ | Pump-out (*not Sat*). Boat
hire, gas, boat building, boat and engine
repairs, mooring, toilets, winter storage.

Ⓑ **The Tewkesbury Yacht Marina**
Bredon rd. (Tewkesbury 293737) Ⓡ Ⓢ Ⓦ Ⓟ Ⓓ
Pump-out. Gas, boat building and repairs,
mooring, chandlery, toilets, showers, winter
storage. *Closed Sat afternoons and Sun.*

Ⓑ **Sovereign Marine Holidays** King
John's Island North, Tewkesbury.
(Worcester 27022). Ⓡ Ⓢ Ⓦ Ⓟ Ⓓ
Pump-out. Boat hire, gas, mooring.

Facilities also available at: Avon Lock,
Tewkesbury Ⓦ Strensham Lock Ⓦ

BOAT TRIPS
Telestar Pleasure Cruises 185 Queens
rd, Tewkesbury (294088). Based at Riverside Walk. Public trips daily on 'Avon
Belle'. (Up to 47 passengers).

PUBS & RESTAURANTS
🛏✕ **Royal Hop Pole Hotel.** (Tewkesbury 293236). Riverside moorings. Lunch,
dinner.

🛏✕ **Swan Hotel** High st, Tewkesbury
(293155). Food.

🛏✕ **Plough Hotel** The Cross,
Tewkesbury (292094). Food.

🛏 **Olde Black Bear** High st, Tewkesbury
(292202).

🛏 **Fleet Inn** Twyning.

🛏 **Royal Oak** Bredon.

🛏✕ **Fox & Hounds** Bredon (72377).
Thatched 15thC. Restaurant, garden.

🛏 **Crown Inn** Eckington. Snacks.

🛏 **Bell Inn** Eckington.

River Avon

Evesham

23 miles

The navigation continues to Pershore. There
are moorings, convenient for the main street,
by the recreation ground above Pershore
Lock. It should be remembered that the
Avon above Pershore has shallows and
bends which call for caution and reduced
speed. Note also that the lock chamber at
Fladbury Lock narrows slightly towards the
bottom, and could crush two tightly fitting
boats when locking down. Stop to check
that the lock channel is clear before proceeding down it. The ferry at Hampton
Ferry, Evesham, is rope operated. The ferry-
man will lower the rope if 3 blasts of the
horn are given. Powered craft should then
cross in neutral. There are bad shoals to be
avoided between here and Evesham New
Bridge. Moorings in the town are by the
Workman Gardens on the right bank. A
sharp look-out should be kept for ferry
chains at Offenham. George Billington is
the first of the new Upper Avon Locks.
These must be worked with great care.

Pershore
Worcs. Pop 20,430. Busy town with well-
kept Georgian buildings, set among fruit
farms. The 14thC bridge with its 6 arches
no longer carries traffic. Pershore Abbey,
of Norman origin, has a magnificent lantern
tower, built c.1330. Nearby St Andrew's
Church contains 13thC-15thC work.

Navigation on the River Avon

The Lower and Upper Avon Navigation
Trusts are charities operated almost entirely
by volunteers. Boat crews can help them
to keep down their costs by observing their
rules and requests. They should also be
acquainted with the relevant bye-laws.
Some important do's and don'ts:
Keep right, and comply with warning and
direction signs.
Give way to commercial craft. Power gives
way to sail.
Maximum speed- 10mph, Lower Avon
(Tewkesbury to Evesham Lock). 4mph,
Upper Avon (Evesham Lock to Stratford).
Do not create a wash which could damage
river banks or other craft.
Always reduce speed when passing moored
craft, and treat anglers with respect.
Moor only at recognised mooring sites.
Never dispose of sewage or refuse into the
river.

Keep off private land.
Keep away from weirs and slow down
when approaching locks.
Never use lock-gates, landing stages etc.
to stop a boat. Use your engine.
Be patient and courteous at locks.
Maximum craft sizes are: Length 70ft.
Beam 13ft 6ins. Draught 3ft 6ins. Head-
room 10ft.
For further details of river use and naviga-
tion charges, contact:
*Lower Avon Navigation Trust, Gable End,
The Holloway, Pershore, Worcs. Pershore
2517.* (Avon Lock, Tewkesbury to Evesham
Lock).
*Upper Avon Navigation Trust, Avon House,
Harvington, Evesham, Worcs. Evesham
870526.* (Evesham Lock to Alveston
Sluice, Stratford-on-Avon).
Both the above produce their own
excellent guides to the river.

Eckington Bridge, Lower Avon. *Derek Pratt.*

Evesham (cont)

Fladbury
Worcs. PO, tel, stores. Picturesque village, once the home of William Sandys who started making the Avon navigable in 1636. Graycombe House, the home of George Perrott who purchased the Lower Avon in the 18thC, is about 1m upriver from the village on the left bank.

Cropthorne
Worcs. Store. A tourist attraction. The village is surrounded by orchards.

Wood Norton
Above the left bank at Chadbury Lock. Once the seat of the Duke of Orleans, it now houses an engineering school run by the B.B.C.

Abbey Manor
1m above Chadbury Lock, on the left. An obelisk in the grounds overlooks Green Hill, site of the Battle of Evesham in 1265, where Simon de Montfort, Earl of Leicester, was killed. Another memorial is the Leicester Tower, built c.1840. Home of the Rudge family.

Evesham
Worcs. Pop 13,850. EC Wed. All services. Centre of the fruit-growing industry. Fine Georgian houses, some half-timbered buildings. Only the gateway and Bell Tower remain of the 14thC Abbey. All Saints', 12thC and St Lawrence's, rebuilt 16thC, are fine churches. Regatta held *every Spring hol Mon.*

The Almonry Museum Vine st. Medieval remains and old agricultural implements. *Open most afternoons.*

Information Evesham Town Council, 110 High st, Evesham (45944).

Offenham
Worcs. EC Sat. PO, tel, stores, Maypole. The church of St Mary and St Milburgh was largely rebuilt in the 19thC.

Salford Priors
Worcs. EC Thur. PO, stores. St Matthew's Church was restored in the 19thC.

Cleeve Prior
Worcs. EC Thur. PO, stores, tel. See church of St Andrew.

BOATYARDS & FACILITIES
ⓑ **Millside Boatyard** 37a Bridge st, Pershore (2849) [W][P][D] Slipway, gas, boat & engine repairs, mooring, chandlery, toilets, winter storage.

ⓑ **Sankey Marine** Worcester rd, Evesham (2338) [W][P][D] Chandlery, boat sales & outboard, moorings, slipway.

ⓑ **Weir Meadow Caravan Park and Boating Station** Lower Leys, Evesham (2417) [R][S][W] Slipway, gas, mooring, chandlery, toilets, showers, winter storage. *Restricted opening in winter.*

ⓑ **Abbots Salford Marine** (Evesham 870244). [W] Moorings, supplies, gas. *Closed Nov–Feb.*

Facilities also available at:
Wyre Mill (Wyre Lock) [W]
Evesham Borough Moorings [W]
Evesham Lock [W]
George Billington Lock [R][S][W]

PUBS & RESTAURANTS
🍺✗ **Angel Inn** Pershore (2046). Restaurant. Moorings, garden.

🍺✗ **Star Inn** Bridge st, Pershore. Grill room, snacks. Moorings, garden.

🍺 **Manor House** Bridge st, Pershore.

🍺 **Anchor Inn** Wyre. Food. Moorings.

✗! **Riverdale** Fladbury, near Jubilee Bridge. Restaurant. Overnight moorings, water.

🍺✗ **Northwick Arms Hotel** Waterside, Evesham (6109). Grill and Buttery. Moorings opposite.

🍺✗ **Evesham Hotel** Coopers lane, Evesham (6344). Restaurant. Garden. Moorings opposite.

✗! **Marine Ballroom & Restaurant** (6068). Lunch/dinner. Moorings. Cater for parties, hire steamers etc. for functions.

🍺✗ **Bridge Inn & Ferry** Offenham. [R] Restaurant, snacks. Moorings.

🍺 **Fish & Anchor** By George Billington Lock.

🍺✗ **Coach & Horses** Harvington, opposite church. Restaurant.

🍺 **The Bell** Salford Priors.

🍺✗ **Kings Arms** Cleeve Prior.

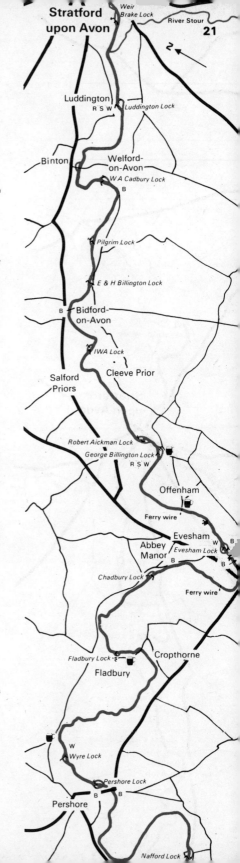

Weir
Brake Lock
River Stour
Luddington
R S W   Luddington Lock
Binton
Welford-on-Avon
W A Cadbury Lock
B
Pilgrim Lock
E & H Billington Lock
B   Bidford-on-Avon
IWA Lock
Salford Priors
Cleeve Prior
Robert Aickman Lock
George Billington Lock
R S W
Offenham
Ferry wire
Evesham
Abbey Manor
W   B
Evesham Lock
B
B
Chadbury Lock
Ferry wire
Cropthorne
Fladbury Lock
Fladbury
W
Wyre Lock
Pershore Lock
B   B
Pershore
Nafford Lock

River Avon

Stratford-upon-Avon

10 miles

Moorings are conveniently situated along the river for villages, supplies, services and pubs; there are also many fine walks. Welford can be reached by crossing the weir (on foot) only when the water level is low. The stretch above Welford is particularly beautiful, passing under the random stone-arched Binton Bridges and on by over-hanging trees to Luddington. Weir Brake Lock takes the river down into Stratford. It was from here that the Queen Mother travelled by narrow boat to Stratford Lock for the Navigation opening ceremony in June 1974. The Stratford-on-Avon Canal joins the Avon at the basin opposite the Royal Shakespeare Theatre. It is possible to cruise 3 miles above Stratford. Do not attempt to go beyond the official end of the Navigation.

Bidford-on-Avon
Warwicks. EC Thur. PO, tel, stores, bank. Threatened by traffic. The church of St Lawrence, originally 13thC, was replaced during the 19thC. The Falcon Inn, which Shakespeare was reputed to frequent, still stands but is empty.

Welford-on-Avon
Warwicks. EC Mon. PO, tel, stores. The church of St Peter is of Norman and early English origin. A pleasant riverside walk leads to Weston-on-Avon whose church of All Saints is well worth a visit.

Luddington
Warwicks. Tel. Eggs are available at Boddington Farm, Main st, by the village green.

Stratford-upon-Avon See p. 69.

BOATYARDS & FACILITIES

Ⓑ **Bidford Boats** Riverside House, 4 The Pleck, Bidford-on-Avon (3205) Ⓢ Ⓦ Hire cruisers, moorings, slipways.

Western Cruisers Western rd, Stratford-on-Avon (69636) Ⓡ Ⓢ Ⓦ Ⓓ Pump-out *(Mar–Oct).* Boat hire, gas, boat & engine repairs, mooring, chandlery, toilets, showers, bread and milk.

Ⓑ **Stratford-upon-Avon Marine** Clopton Bridge, Stratford-on-Avon (69669/ 69773) Ⓡ Ⓢ Ⓦ Ⓓ Pump-out. Gas, chandlery, boat hire, boat building & repairs, mooring, toilets, showers, restaurant. *Closed Sat afternoon & Sun in winter.*

Facilities also available at: Luddington Ⓡ Ⓢ Ⓦ

PUBS & RESTAURANTS

Ⓟ **Bull's Head** High st, Bidford. Snacks.
Ⓟ✕ **Four Alls** Binton Bridges, Welford. Restaurant.
Ⓟ **The Shakespeare** Chapel st, Welford.
Ⓟ **Cottage of Content** Near the river, opposite E & H Billington Lock. Plenty of pubs and restaurants in Stratford-on-Avon. See p. 69.

BCN

Maximum dimensions

Length: 71' 6"
Beam: 7'
Headroom: 6' 6"

Mileages

Birmingham Canal new main line
BIRMINGHAM Gas Street to
SMETHWICK JUNCTION (old main
line): $2\frac{7}{8}$
BROMFORD JUNCTION: $4\frac{7}{8}$
PUDDING GREEN JUNCTION
(Wednesbury Old Canal): $5\frac{5}{8}$
TIPTON FACTORY JUNCTION (old
main line): $8\frac{3}{8}$
DEEPFIELDS JUNCTION (Wednesbury
Oak Loop): 10
Bradley Workshops: $2\frac{1}{4}$
HORSELEY FIELDS JUNCTION
(Wyrley & Essington Canal): 13
Wolverhampton top lock: $13\frac{1}{2}$
ALDERSLEY JUNCTION
(Staffordshire & Worcestershire Canal): $15\frac{1}{8}$

Total 24 locks (3 up, 21 down)

Birmingham Canal old main line
SMETHWICK JUNCTION to
Junction with Engine Branch: $\frac{1}{2}$
SPON LANE JUNCTION: $1\frac{1}{2}$
OLDBURY JUNCTION (Titford Canal): $2\frac{1}{2}$
BRADES HALL JUNCTION (Gower
Branch): $3\frac{1}{2}$
Aqueduct over Netherton Tunnel
branch: $4\frac{3}{8}$
TIPTON JUNCTION (Dudley Canal): $5\frac{1}{2}$
FACTORY JUNCTION (new main line): 6

Total 3 locks

Dudley Canal line no. 1
TIPTON JUNCTION to
Dudley Tunnel (north end): $\frac{3}{8}$
PARK HEAD JUNCTION: $2\frac{3}{8}$
Black Delph bottom lock (Stourbridge
Canal): $4\frac{1}{2}$

Total 12 locks

Dudley Canal line no. 2
PARK HEAD JUNCTION to
WINDMILL END JUNCTION: $2\frac{5}{8}$
COOMBESWOOD BASIN: $5\frac{1}{2}$

No locks

Netherton Tunnel Branch
WINDMILL END JUNCTION to
DUDLEY PORT JUNCTION: $2\frac{7}{8}$

No locks

Wednesbury Old Canal
PUDDING GREEN JUNCTION to
RYDER'S GREEN JUNCTION: $\frac{5}{8}$

No locks

Walsall Canal
RYDER'S GREEN JUNCTION to
Ryder's Green bottom lock: $\frac{3}{4}$
TAME VALLEY JUNCTION: $1\frac{3}{4}$
Junction with Anson Branch (for Bentley
Canal): $5\frac{1}{4}$
WALSALL JUNCTION: $6\frac{7}{8}$

Total 8 locks

Walsall Branch Canal
WALSALL JUNCTION to
BIRCHILLS JUNCTION (Wyrley &
Essington Canal): $\frac{7}{8}$

Total 8 locks

Wyrley & Essington Canal
HORSELEY FIELDS JUNCTION to
WEDNESFIELD JUNCTION (Bentley
Canal): $1\frac{1}{4}$
SNEYD JUNCTION: $6\frac{1}{4}$
BIRCHILLS JUNCTION (Walsall Branch
Canal): 8
PELSALL JUNCTION (Cannock
Extension): $12\frac{7}{8}$
Norton Canes Docks: 2
CATSHILL JUNCTION: $15\frac{3}{8}$
OGLEY JUNCTION (Anglesey
Branch): $16\frac{3}{8}$
Anglesey Basin and Chasewater: $1\frac{1}{2}$

No locks

Daw End Branch
CATSHILL JUNCTION to
LONGWOOD JUNCTION (Rushall top
lock): $5\frac{1}{4}$

No locks

Rushall Canal
LONGWOOD JUNCTION to
RUSHALL JUNCTION: $2\frac{3}{4}$

Total 9 locks

Tame Valley Canal
TAME VALLEY JUNCTION to
RUSHALL JUNCTION: $3\frac{1}{2}$
Perry Barr top lock: $5\frac{1}{2}$
SALFORD JUNCTION: $8\frac{1}{2}$

Total 13 locks

Titford Canal
OLDBURY LOCKS JUNCTION to
CAUSEWAY GREEN: $1\frac{1}{2}$

Total 6 locks

The Birmingham Canal Company was authorised in 1768 to build a canal from Aldersley on the Staffordshire & Worcestershire Canal to Birmingham. With James Brindley as engineer the work proceeded very fast. The first section, from Birmingham to the Wednesbury collieries, was opened in November 1769, and the whole 22½-mile route was completed in 1772. It was a winding, contour canal, with twelve locks taking it over Smethwick, and another twenty (later 21) taking it down through Wolverhampton to Aldersley Junction. As the route of the canal was through an area of mineral wealth and developing industry, its success was immediate. Pressure of traffic caused the summit level at Smethwick to be lowered in the 1790s (thus cutting out 6 locks – 3 on either side of the summit), and during the same period branches began to reach out towards Walsall via the Ryder's Green Locks, and towards Fazeley. Out of this very profitable and ambitious first main line, there grew the Birmingham Canal Navigations, more commonly abbreviated to BCN. After a long dispute about the building of the canal from Birmingham to Fazeley, the Birmingham Company bought up the embryonic Birmingham & Fazeley Canal Company; in 1794 the cumbersome title created by this merger, 'The Birmingham and Birmingham & Fazeley Canal Company', was changed to the simpler BCN. The battle for the right to build the Fazeley line was long and hard, and was fought with considerable intrigue and bitterness, a pattern of behaviour that tended to surround all the activities of the Birmingham Company. Being first in the field, it generally behaved in a high-handed manner, holding the whip hand over rivals when extensions and developments were proposed. Generally it exacted high compensatory tolls, and exercised strict controls over water rights – habits that pleased the shareholders but infuriated competitors.

The BCN network that exists today developed from three rival companies each seeking to capture traffic from the others. This intense competition resulted in a very intricate network, which was thus able to cater for all the material and distribution needs of the developing industries in the area. The web of lines forming the BCN became the veins of the Black Country, carrying the life blood of its commerce and wealth.

Apart from the Birmingham Company, there were two other companies instrumental in the creation of the BCN network. Over the other side of the Rowley Hills, the Dudley and Stourbridge Companies had set up a rival route to the Staffs & Worcs, to the annoyance of the Birmingham Company. Thomas Dadford, who had worked with Brindley earlier, was appointed engineer, and in three years (1776–9) it was completed as planned to a point just below the present Blower's Green Lock. Immediately there were plans to extend it underground to link with Lord Ward's private canal, and with the Birmingham at Tipton. After several setbacks this extension was completed between 1785 and 1792, including the long Dudley Tunnel. Then once again the direct-

ness of the Dudley company prompted it to undertake a further extension to link with the recently authorised Worcester & Birmingham Canal at Selly Oak, a means of avoiding the severe compensation tolls exacted by the Birmingham Company for the junction at Tipton. This new line, eleven miles long, was opened in 1798. It included two tunnels, that at Lappal being the fifth longest in Britain. Cut through rock strata with great difficulty, this tunnel suffered continuously from subsidence and roof falls, and had to undergo frequent closure for repairs. The financial strain of this last extension nearly crippled the Dudley Company, and it only just managed to survive until 1846, when it was absorbed by the BCN. Lappal Tunnel was finally closed in 1917.

Up in the north, the Wyrley & Essington Company joined the fray, completing a line from Wolverhampton to Wyrley in 1795 under the direction of William Pitt. This company also grew quickly, extending the canal first to Brownhills, and then to join the Coventry Canal at Huddlesford via the Ogley flight of thirty locks. Several branches were added to serve the rich coalfields around Cannock and Brownhills, which were destined to serve the BCN and West Midlands well when the Black Country pits began to decline. Indeed the meandering line of the Wyrley & Essington saw some of the last commercial traffic on the whole BCN network. The Birmingham Company had spread northwards to Walsall, but because of ill-feeling and rivalry, the logical link with the Wyrley & Essington line was not made until 1840, when the Walsall Branch Canal was built.

Traffic continued to increase, and with it the wealth of the BCN. The pressures of trade made the main line at Smethwick very congested, and brought grave problems of water supply. Steam pumping engines were installed in several places to recirculate the water, and the company appointed Thomas Telford to shorten Brindley's old main line. Between 1825 and 1838 he engineered a new main line between Deepfields and Birmingham, using massive cuttings and embankments to maintain a continuous level. These improvements not only increased the amount of available waterway (the old line remaining in use), but also shortened the route from Birmingham to Wolverhampton by seven miles.

Serious congestion had also arisen at Farmer's Bridge Locks, which could not keep up with the traffic although they operated 24 hours a day and 7 days a week. Land was not available for a duplicate flight in the immediate area, and so an earlier plan to build a canal following the valley of the River Tame was revived. However, it was not until railway control and amalgamation with the Wyrley & Essington had come in 1840 that the necessary impetus came to promote the Tame Valley Canal, and the whole series of extensions and improvements to the network that accompanied it. These developments led to the building of a relief for the narrow Dudley Tunnel: the Netherton Tunnel, cut on a parallel course, included a towpath on each side and gas lighting throughout. The last addition to the network was the Cannock Extension Canal to Hednesford Basin, with its link to the Staffs & Worcs Canal via Churchbridge Locks.

Railway control of the BCN meant an expansion of the use of the system, and a large number of interchange basins were built to promote outside trade by means of rail traffic. This was of course quite contrary to the usual effect of railway competition upon canals. Trade continued to grow in relation to industrial development, and by the end of the 19thC it was topping 8½ million tons per annum. A large proportion of this trade was local, being dependent upon the needs and output of Black Country industry. After the turn of the century this reliance on local trade started the gradual decline of the system as deposits of raw materials became exhausted. Factories bought from further afield, and developed along the railways and roads away from the canals. Yet as late as 1950 there was over a million tons of trade, and the system continued in operation until the abrupt end of the coal trade in 1966, a pattern quite different from canals as a whole.

As trade declined, so parts of the system fell out of use and were abandoned. At its heyday in 1865, the BCN comprised over 160 miles of canal. Today just over 100 miles survive, and of these some 65 are without a guaranteed future, being classed as 'Remainder Waterways'. However, all the surviving canals of the BCN are of great interest; although not ideal for leisure cruising, they represent a most vivid example of living history, one of the most important monuments to the industrial revolution.

The report of the official working party of 1970 indicates the value of the surviving BCN network for amenity and water supply purposes, and, at the same time, points to the enormous cost of eliminating the 'Remainder' sections; as always, restoration is cheaper than removal. The work on the reopening of the Dudley Tunnel line, Park Head Locks and the Titford Canal shows the increasing local council interest in canals as a whole, and their concern for urban recreational facilities. If this pattern is to continue, then the future of this unique network would seem secure.

BCN Main Line

15⅛ miles

The Main Line of the Birmingham Canal Navigations (BCN) starts from Worcester Bar Basin, usually known as Gas Street Basin. This is a remarkably authentic canal settlement, with moored narrow boats in working trim a stark contrast to the rest of Birmingham.
The main line passes immediately under Broad Street Bridge (almost a tunnel) and on to Farmers Bridge Junction, a canal 'crossroads'. To the right is the Birmingham & Fazeley Canal heading NE to Salford Junction. A short distance along here, near the top lock, is the Cambrian Wharf development, a restored basin with a canal-side walk, two terraces of 18thC cottages and a pub, the 'Long Boat', with many canal relics; one of the bars is a converted narrow boat. To the left of the 'crossroads' is the Oozells Street Loop, the first of three loops that mark the original contour route of Brindley's old main line. The new main line, built by Telford, continues straight ahead to be rejoined in a short while by the Oozells Street Loop coming in from the left. The canal is flanked by factories and warehouses all with their backs turned to the waterway, leaving it strangely isolated from the rest of the city.
The Icknield Port Loop branches to the left and rejoins at another 'crossroads' where the Soho Loop, the largest of the three, sweeps round to the right for over a mile. At the point where it rejoins the main line there is an island in the middle of the canal, site of one of the many toll offices that existed throughout the system.
Ignored by the factories and warehouses, the main line continues on to Smethwick Junction. Here the old course forks right up three locks; the new course forks left keeping level. The two routes run side by side, the old above the new, their banks forming an unofficial nature reserve amidst the industry and dereliction, with wild flowers and black-berry bushes growing in profusion. The Engine Arm that leaves the old line and crosses over the new is a short feeder canal, its name coming from a Boulton & Watt steam pumping engine that fed the old

Smethwick Locks 20'0"
Smethwick Junction

Birmingham Canal Main Line

Soho Loop

Rotton Park Reservoir

Icknield Port Loop
BWB Yard

West Bromwich

W & B (see p. 78)

Farmers Bridge Junction

R S W

Gas St Basin B

Birmingham & Fazeley

Tame Valley Canal

Salford Junction

Saltley Canal

B & F (see p. 33)

Birmingham

The Birmingham Canal Main Line passes through a heavily industrialised and built up area. The many bridges have been omitted in order that they should not obscure the map.

Grand Union (see p. 48)

summit level of the BCN for 120 years. It was then moved to Ocker Hill to pump water from disused mine workings before it retired in the 1950's to rest in the Birmingham Museum of Science & Industry. By forking right at Spon Lane Junction, the navigator on the old main line can switch to the new if he wishes a canal 'slip road' locks down to the newer route, overshadowed by the motorway. These three Spon Lane Locks are believed to be the oldest working locks in the country. The left fork follows the old route, crossing Telfords new line via the Stewart Aqueduct. It is worth noting that the new line after Bromford Junction is particularly straight, singularly dull and closely escorted by the main electrified railway.

At Pudding Green Junction (new main line) the Walsall Canal leaves to the right to join the Tame Valley and Wyrley & Essington Canals through a mass of industry.

At Oldbury Junction (old main line) the recently restored Titford Canal branches to the left to Titford Pool. The Gower Branch links the new line to the old between junctions Albion and Bradeshall.

The entrance to Netherton Tunnel can be seen to the south from Dudley Port Junction (new main line), this leads to the Dudley Canal and the SW. At Tipton Junction (old main line) the branch to the left leads to the Dudley Tunnel, the right to Factory Junction where the old and new main lines rejoin to continue on through the factories and industrial wastelands towards Wolverhampton. Deepfields Junction is reached after passing through Telford's Coseley Tunnel. The Wednesbury Oak Loop joins here from the right. This is part of Brindley's old route, now a two mile blind alley with a BWB maintenance yard at the end. North of the junction the canal winds through Wolverhampton, unaltered by Telford.

At Horseley Fields Junction the Wyrley & Essington Canal heads off NE on its tortuous route to Brownhills. It used to join the Coventry Canal at Huddlesford but now ends at Ogley Junction. The main line descends the 21 locks of the Wolverhampton flight to Aldersley Junction and the Staffordshire & Worcestershire Canal. The change of surroundings here is quite dramatic, from industry at the top of the flight to virtual countryside at the bottom. Access throughout the BCN is bad to visit shops or a pub usually involves scaling walls. Leaving your boat unattended is not a good idea due to the likelihood of vandalism. The waterways have been used as unofficial rubbish tips for years, and navigators with fibre glass hulls to their boats should proceed with the utmost caution. It goes without saying that old ropes and polythene sacks will foul your propeller. Not everyone's cup of tea, but a vivid relic of the Industrial Revolution.

The Birmingham Canal Main Line passes through a heavily industrialised and built up area. The many bridges have been omitted in order that they should not obscure the map.

Waterways of the BCN

Of the 100 odd miles of BCN waterway that are still open to navigation today, only six actually fall within the area of the City of Birmingham. The remainder of the surviving canals interlace nine local authority areas, and play a correspondingly vital role in industrial water supply and land drainage. Serving as arteries through the Black Country, the canals have an enormous recreational potential, although there is little commercial traffic using the network today. With the exception of the Birmingham Main Line, the Stourbridge and Birmingham & Fazeley lines, and Netherton Tunnel, all the BCN is classed as 'remainder waterway'. In the report of the Birmingham Canal Navigations Working Party, published in 1970, it was recommended that much of the surviving network be promoted to 'cruising waterway' status, to ensure that the canals play their part in the developing leisure amenities for Birmingham and the Midlands generally.

Cruising the BCN is an unusual, and often dramatic, experience; the canals provide a continuous panorama of the history of the Black Country, and of the Industrial Revolution. There are frequent reminders of the importance of the canals in the development of the area, the toll islands isolated in the middle of the canal, the railway interchange basins, the factory arms and basins, often revealed today only by the arch of the towpath bridge buried in the brickwork, the loading bays of the factories which at one time were totally dependent upon the canals, the engine houses (the best example near the south portal of Netherton Tunnel), and the disused and abandoned arms and branches, some closed so long ago that their course is now difficult to trace. Although industry has turned its back on the BCN, the canals are far from derelict or depressing. Scattered among the older buildings are new developments, many of which accept the canal as a natural part of the landscape. Cambrian Wharf is the obvious example, but in a different way the motorway interchange (commonly known as 'Spaghetti Junction'), built in the air above Salford Junction and the Tame Valley Canal, and the Post Office tower that dominates Farmer's Bridge Locks are equally impressive. Not all the BCN is built up and industrial. For most of its length the Wyrley & Essington is a rural canal, following a winding contour line. The Rushall Canal and the Daw End Branch are also largely undeveloped, offering a quiet alternative to the busy Birmingham Main Line. Even the industrial stretches are often quiet and remote, enjoying the isolation imposed on them by the end of commercial traffic. Kestrels now hover above the waters of the Walsall Canal.

The guide does not cover all the BCN in the usual scale, and so details of many of the features that make up the BCN network are given alphabetically below.

Anglesey Branch

The branch leaves the Wyrley & Essington Canal at Ogley Junction, and runs north-west to Chasewater. It is predominantly a rural canal, passing through heathland before ending in the wide basin, overshadowed by the dam that contains the reservoir. Despite its rural nature, this canal saw the last regular coal traffic on the BCN, carrying coal from the Cannock mines until 1967. The course of the railway that used to serve the basin, and the remains of the loading wharves, can still be traced without difficulty. The branch is the ideal approach to the pleasure park that now surrounds the reservoir.

Bentley Canal

Built after 1840 as an additional link between the Walsall and the Wyrley & Essington Canals, little of the Bentley is now usable. Its eastern end is cut by a motorway, and survives mainly as a feeder for Walsall power station. The western end exists for six locks after Wednesfield Junction, but the rest of the canal has been converted into a water channel.

Cannock Extension Canal

Opened in 1858, the Cannock Extension was built to serve the coalmines of Cannock Chase. It was the last BCN Canal to be built, and it was also one of the last to carry regular commercial traffic. As built it ran in a straight line to Churchbridge Locks which linked it with the Staffs & Worcs Canal, but the northern half has vanished completely beneath the A5 and the neighbouring coalfields. It now serves Norton Canes Docks, a centre for narrow boat building and maintenance. Despite its recent industrial past, the Cannock Extension is totally rural; heath and woodland surround it, and there are few buildings to be seen. The water is clear, the towpath rich in wild flowers. The late building of the canal is revealed by its straightness, and by the distinctive blue brick bridges.

Dudley Canal

The Dudley Canal, whose history is intimately involved with that of the Stourbridge Canal, was built in several stages. Today it survives only in truncated form, but still serves as the vital link between the BCN and the west of England via the Staffs & Worcs Canal. The canal starts at the eight Black Delph Locks, which were rebuilt in 1858. The old locks can be seen to the west of the present flight. The surroundings are largely industrial, but these are often exciting; the canal passes right through Round Oak steelworks at Brierley Hill. Parkhead Locks, reopened in 1973, lead to Dudley Tunnel (see below). From Parkhead Junction the canal continues eastwards along a meandering contour line which takes it round Netherton Hill, dominated by the tower of Netherton Church. Much of the land around the canal is now heath and waste land, and so there are good views to the south. After the short Bumblehole branch, where one yard keeps alive a long tradition of boatbuilding, the canal divides at Windmill End Junction. The northern line leads to Netherton Tunnel, the southern to Hawne Basin. Originally this line continued in a

Continued on page 30

The BCN network

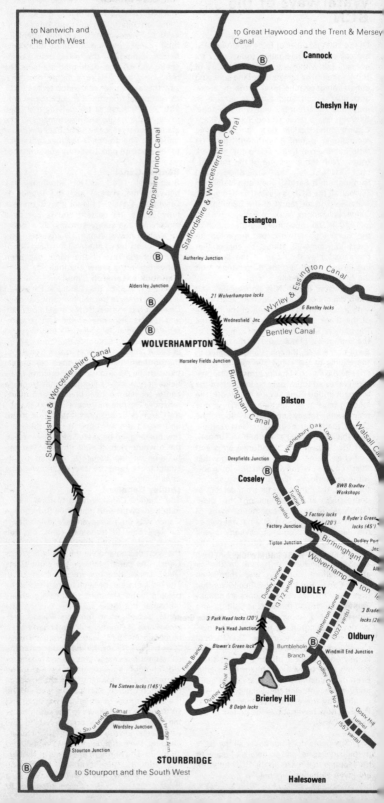

to Nantwich and the North West

to Great Haywood and the Trent & Mersey Canal

Ⓑ Cannock

Cheshyn Hay

Shropshire Union Canal

Staffordshire & Worcestershire Canal

Essington

Wyrley & Essington Canal

Ⓑ Autherley Junction

Aldersley Junction Ⓑ

21 Wolverhampton locks

6 Bentley locks

Wednesfield Jnc

Ⓑ

Bentley Canal

WOLVERHAMPTON

Horseley Fields Junction

Staffordshire & Worcestershire Canal

Birmingham Canal

Bilston

Walsall Ca

Wednesbury Oak Loop

Deepfields Junction

Coseley Ⓑ

BWB Bradley Workshops

Coseley Tunnel (360 yards)

3 Factory locks (20')

8 Ryder's Green locks (45')

Factory Junction

Tipton Junction

Birmingham

Dudley Port Jnc

Wolverhampton le

All

Dudley Tunnel (3172 yards)

DUDLEY

Netherton Tunnel (3027 yards)

3 Brade locks (26

3 Park Head locks (20')

Park Head Junction

Fens Branch

Blower's Green lock

Bumblehole Branch

Windmill End Junction Ⓑ

Oldbury

The Sixteen locks (145')

Dudley Canal No 1

Dudley Canal No 2

Gosty Hill Tunnel (557 yards)

8 Delph locks

Brierley Hill

Stourbridge Canal

Stourbridge Arm

Wordsley Junction

Ⓑ Stourton Junction

STOURBRIDGE

to Stourport and the South West

Halesowen

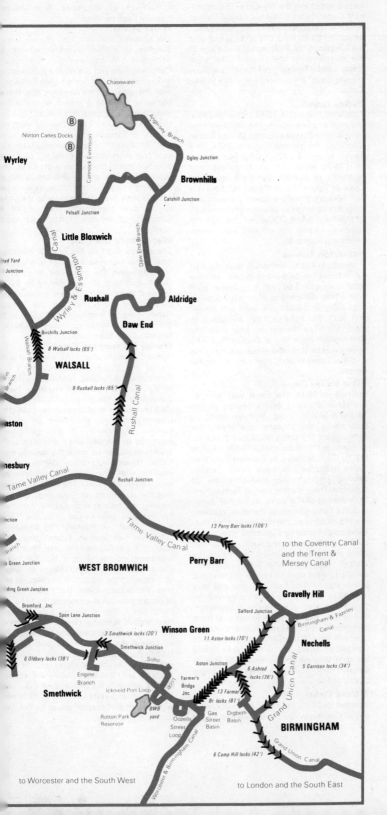

Chasewater

Anglesey Branch

Norton Canes Docks

Wyrley

Cannock Extension

Ogley Junction

Brownhills

Catshill Junction

Pelsall Junction

Daw End Branch

Little Bloxwich

Canal

...yd Yard
...Junction

Wyrley & Essington

Rushall

Aldridge

Daw End

Birchills Junction

8 Walsall locks (65')

Walsall Branch

WALSALL

9 Rushall locks (65')

...n
Branch

...aston

Rushall Canal

...nesbury

Tame Valley Canal

Rushall Junction

...ction

Tame Valley Canal

13 Perry Barr locks (106')

to the Coventry Canal
and the Trent &
Mersey Canal

...ranch

...s Green Junction

WEST BROMWICH

Perry Barr

Gravelly Hill

...ding Green Junction

Bromford Jnc

Spon Lane Junction

Salford Junction

Birmingham & Fazeley Canal

3 Smethwick locks (20')

Winson Green

11 Aston locks (70')

Nechells

6 Oldbury locks (38')

Smethwick Junction

Soho

Aston Junction

6 Ashted locks (36')

5 Garrison locks (34')

Engine
Branch

BCN

Farmer's
Bridge
Jnc

13 Farmer's
Br locks (81')

Grand Union Canal

Smethwick

Icknield Port Loop

BIRMINGHAM

BWB
yard

Rotton Park
Reservoir

Oozells
Street
Loop

Gas
Street
Basin

Digbeth
Basin

Worcester & Birmingham Canal

6 Camp Hill locks (42')

Grand Union Canal

to Worcester and the South West

to London and the South East

wide circle to join the Worcester & Birmingham Canal via the notorious Lappal Tunnel, which was closed in 1917 because of subsidence. 3,795yds long, this rocky tunnel was the longest in the BCN network and one of the narrowest in the country. The short Gosty Hill Tunnel (577yds) precedes Hawne Basin, the present end of the Dudley Canal.

Dudley Tunnel
Reopened to boats in 1973 (although petrol or diesel engines must not be used) with the rebuilding of Parkhead Locks, Dudley Tunnel is one of the wonders of the BCN. This narrow tunnel, 3,172yds long, was opened in 1792, after the usual delays and problems, to connect with the Birmingham Canal at Tipton. Inside the tunnel there is a vast network of natural caverns, basins and branches serving old quarries and mines. In all there are over 5,000yds of underground waterway, some cut off and abandoned, others still accessible.

Netherton Tunnel
Opened in 1858, Netherton was the last canal tunnel to be built in Britain, and the most luxurious. 3,027yds long, it was built with a bore sufficient to allow a towpath on both sides, and when opened it was equipped with gas lighting, later converted to electricity. The Netherton line joins the Birmingham main line at Dudley Port. The tunnel was built to relieve congestion in the Dudley Tunnel, and runs on a parallel course.

Tame Valley Canal
Opened in 1844, the canal was built to overcome the long delays caused by the Farmer's Bridge Locks. With towpaths on both banks, this straight canal leaves the Birmingham & Fazeley at Salford Junction, its north westerly course overshadowed at first by the motorway. As it climbs Perry Barr Locks it comes into more open country, passing through the gradual stages of suburbia. There is a fine view of Birmingham from the top of the locks. At Rushall Junction the canal swings to the west, crossing the M5 motorway, the railway and the river Tame on one great embankment. Its elevated course continues as the surroundings become more industrial, and finally it joins the Walsall Canal at Tame Valley Junction, dwarfed by the cooling towers of Ocker Hill power station. The Rushall Canal was built in 1847 to connect the Tame Valley with the Daw End branch of the Wyrley & Essington, and thus to capture some of the coal trade from the Cannock mines. It continues the northern line of the Tame Valley Canal to Longwood Junction, the nine locks raising the canal through open country. The Rushall Canal is well known to anglers for its ample stocks of fish.

Titford Canal
Opened in 1837, the canal climbed originally to Causeway Green via six locks. Today it survives in shortened form having recently been restored.

Walsall Canal
The Walsall Canal runs from Ryder's Green Junction to Birchills Junction, making an alternative link between the Birmingham Canal main line and the Wyrley & Essington. It connects with the Tame Valley Canal and with the remains of the Bentley Canal. It was started in 1786 as a branch from the Birmingham line to serve Walsall, but did not reach Walsall until 1799. The link with the Wyrley & Essington was not made until 1841 because of company rivalry, but in that year the short Walsall Branch Canal was built to connect the two via eight locks. The course of the Walsall Canal is largely industrial, with a large number of basins, wharves and old arms. Despite the industry the canal is now quiet and remote, for much of its surroundings are now derelict and abandoned.

Wednesbury Old Canal
The specification for the original Birmingham Canal included a branch to Wednesbury, to leave the main line at Pudding Green Junction. It was opened in 1769. Today it serves as a vital link between the Birmingham main line and the Walsall Canal, while its original course survives as the Ridgeacre branch, continuing eastward towards West Bromwich.

Wyrley & Essington Canal
Opened throughout in 1797, the canal connected the Birmingham Canal with the Birmingham & Fazeley, running in a meandering contour line from Horseley Field Junction to Huddlesford, via Lichfield. From Huddlesford it was able to connect with the Coventry, Oxford and Trent & Mersey Canals. The Wyrley & Essington was prompted by the coal trade, and there were several branches to serve the various coal fields. However its trade did not really develop until the Cannock fields were exploited in the 19thC. The most important was the Hay Head (or Daw End) Branch running southwards from Catshill Junction; for this was later linked with the Tame Valley Canal via Rushall. The Wyrley & Essington was built as a rural canal, and today this is still largely the case. Most of its wandering course takes it through heath and woodland, although there are continual reminders of the industrial heritage of the area. The water is clear, and a great variety of plants grow on the towpath. In 1954 the main line between Ogley Junction and Huddlesford was abandoned, and much of this has now completely vanished, although its course through Lichfield and west of Huddlesford can still be traced. Today the canal ends abruptly at Ogley, but its connections with the Tame Valley and Walsall Canals, and with the Birmingham main line make it an important part of the BCN network, a part that is emphasised by the rural nature of the canal.

RESTAURANTS

✕❢ **Burlington Restaurant** Burlington Passage, New street, Birmingham. (021 643 3081). Basement restaurant offering a mixture of English and continental food.

✕❢ **Copper Kettle** 151 Milcote road, Bearwood, Birmingham. (021 429 7920) Excellent French-inspired menu. *Closed Sun, Mon, Tue and all Aug.*

✕❢ **La Capanna** Hurst street, Birmingham. (021 622 2287). Italian food, imaginative and ever changing menu. *Closed Sun and B. Hols.*

✕❢ **Danish Food Centre** Stephenson Place, Birmingham. (021 643 2837). Useful Danish restaurant, open all day, from 8.00–22.30. Good mixture of hot and cold dishes, draught lager. *Closed Sun.*

🍲 ✕ **Long Boat** Cambrian wharf, Kingston row. Canalside. Steak bar.

✕❢ **Salamis Kebab House** 178 Broad street, Birmingham. (021 643 2997). Greek-Cypriot restaurant, near city centre. Customers choose their food in the kitchen.

✕❢ **Rendezvous Restaurant** 40 Berry street, Wolverhampton. (23481). Olde worlde restaurant, with furniture and staff to match. Mixed English and continental menu.

BOATYARDS & BWB

Ⓑ **Canal Transport Services** Norton Canes Docks, Lime lane, Pelsall, Staffs. (Brownhills 4370). On the Cannock Extension Canal. Ⓡ Ⓢ Ⓦ Ⓟ Ⓓ Gas, chandlery, drydock and slipway, moorings, winter storage, boat-building, sales and repairs, inboard and outboard engine sales and repairs.

Ⓑ **M. E. Braine** Norton Canes Docks, Lime lane, Pelsall, Staffs (Brownhills 4888). On the Cannock Extension Canal. Ⓡ Ⓢ Ⓦ Ⓓ Gas, slipway, moorings and winter storage, toilets, boatbuilding and conversions, inboard engine sales and repairs. 46 & 48-seater trip boats for hire to parties. *Closed Sat afternoon and Sun.*

Ⓑ **Alfred Matty** Biddings lane, Deepfields, Coseley, West Midlands. (Bilston 42725). On the BCN main line. Emergency repairs.

Canal Shop & Information Centre 2 Kingston row, Birmingham. (021 236 2645). Chandlery, canal publications and wares for sale, general BWB information and leaflets available. Ⓡ Ⓢ Ⓦ Pump-out. Moorings at Cambrian Wharf administered from here. Toilets, provisions.

Ⓑ **Brummagem Boats** Sherborne Street Wharf. (021 643 8397) Ⓡ Ⓢ Ⓦ Pump-out. Boat hire, gas, boat building & repairs, mooring, chandlery, toilets. *Closed Sun in winter.*

BOAT TRIPS

Dudley Canal Trust Tunnel Trips. For information on trips through the Dudley Tunnel, longest tunnel navigable on the waterways, contact Pat Walker, 30 Mayfield Cres, Rowley Regis, Warley, W. Midlands. (021 559 4464).

Smethwick, Birmingham Canal Old Main Line. *Derek Pratt.*

Stourbridge

The Stourbridge and Dudley Canals are to some extent inseparable, being part of the same grand scheme to link the Dudley coal mines with the Stourbridge glass works, and with the Severn navigation by means of the Staffs & Worcs Canal. After the passing of both Authorisation Acts on the same day in 1776, work was started with Thomas Dadford as engineer. Both canals were soon successful, and decided to increase their revenues by building the Dudley Tunnel and linking with the rich Birmingham traffic. This was opened in 1792 and further strengthened the position of the two companies. In 1840 the Stourbridge Extension Canal was opened linking with the Shut End Collieries. In the middle of the 19thC railway competition began to affect the canal, but it managed to maintain its independence until nationalisation in 1948. Soon after the cessation of carrying, the canal became unnavigable, but was rescued by the joint efforts of the Staffs & Worcs Canal Society and the BWB. In 1967 the canal was re-opened to traffic, with pleasure boats taking the place of the trading boats that had made the Stourbridge Canal so profitable in earlier days.

Maximum dimensions
Length: 70'
Beam: 7'
Headroom: 6'
Mileage
STOURTON JUNCTION to
Wordsley Junction: 2
Stourbridge: 3¼
BLACK DELPH bottom lock: 5¼
Total 16 locks

5¼ miles

Leaving the Staffordshire & Worcestershire Canal at Stourton Junction, the canal climbs four locks past the waterside gardens of Stewpony village at the start of its ascent to Birmingham. As far as Wordsley Junction the canal is rural with only the occasional bridge breaking the seclusion. The Stourbridge Branch heads SE to Stourbridge, the main line begins the 16 lock climb to Leys Junction, where the Fens Branch feeder joins from Pensnett Reservoir (Fens Pools). The Stourbridge Canal ends at Delph bottom lock, the last part of its journey being through industry. From here the Dudley Canal continues on to the tunnels Dudley and Netherton and the BCN Main Line.

Stourbridge
West Midlands. Pop 52,000. EC Thur. MD Fri/Sat. All services. Although the origins of Stourbridge go back to the middle ages, there is little trace of this today. It is almost entirely a 19thC town, reflecting the great expansion of the glass industry during that period. There is one 18thC church, St. Thomas's, and a great variety of Victorian ones.

PUBS
Unicorn Woolaston.
Longlands Tavern Stourbridge.
Foley Arms Brierley Hill.
Vine Brierley Hill.

Birmingham & Fazeley Canal

The Birmingham & Fazeley Canal was authorised in 1784 after a great deal of opposition from the Birmingham Canal Company (who later merged with it). It was built by John Smeeton and completed in 1789. The sponsors knew the canal would be dependent for its success solely on other canals, as it was nothing more than a link route. So at Coleshill in 1782, before its enabling act was passed, they obtained the following agreements. The Oxford Canal Company was to finish its line to Oxford and the Thames; the Coventry Canal Company agreed to extend its line from Atherstone to Fazeley, the new B & F Company building its proposed line and continuing along the defaulting Coventry route from Fazeley to Whittington Brook (see also Coventry Canal history, page 35); and the Trent & Mersey Company pledged to finish the Coventry's line from Whittington Brook to Fradley Junction on the T & M. This joint programme was completed in 1790 and immediately traffic began to flow along the system. Its function as an important link route was soon established and still remains.

Maximum dimensions
Length: 72'
Beam: 7'
Headroom: 7' 6"
Main line
FARMERS BRIDGE JUNCTION (Birmingham Canal) to ASTON JUNCTION (Digbeth Branch): 1½ miles, 13 locks
SALFORD JUNCTION (Tame Valley Canal): 3¼ miles, 24 locks
Minworth Top Lock: 6¼ miles, 24 locks
Curdworth Tunnel: 8½ miles, 27 locks
Bodymoor Heath bridge: 11½ miles, 36 locks
FAZELEY JUNCTION (Coventry Canal): 15 miles, 38 locks
Hopwas: 17¾ miles, 38 locks
Whittington Brook: 20½ miles, 38 locks
Digbeth Branch
ASTON JUNCTION (main line) to DIGBETH Basin: 1 mile, 6 locks

12 miles

The section from Farmers Bridge to Salford Junction is covered in the Worcester & Birmingham section on page 78 of this book. The area covered here starts at Salford Junction under the motorway interchange known almost universally as 'Spaghetti Junction', and runs east through the suburbs of Birmingham, at one point being roofed over for 150 yards by an industrial building. Most factories ignore the canal, except the Cincinnati Works whose landscaped lawns and gardens to the water's edge make a fine exception. Minworth Locks start the descent, which is continued after a short tunnel, by Curdworth Locks. Through Bodymoor Heath the canal is isolated and the surroundings are bleak, although approaching Drayton Bassett, oak trees line the route. The Gothic style footbridge followed by a swivel bridge, lend a welcome note of eccentricity to an otherwise unexciting stretch. At Fazeley Junction, overlooked by a dignified canal house, the Coventry Canal is joined.

Curdworth
Warwicks. Pop 517. PO, tel, stores, garage. In a predominantly industrial area. The squat church is partly Norman; note the finely carved font.
Bodymoor Heath
Warwicks. PO, tel. A scattered village beyond which gravel pits, many flooded and overgrown, break up the fields. Amidst this dereliction are some 18thC buildings, the 'Dog & Doublet' pub being an example worth patronising.
Drayton Bassett
Staffs. EC Mon. PO, tel, stores, fish & chips. Its best feature is the charming and totally unexpected Gothic style footbridge over the canal. Its twin battlemented towers would look quite commanding but for their ridiculously small size. This bridge is unique, and there seems to be no explanation for its eccentricity; greatly increasing its attraction.
Drayton Manor Park & Zoo Alongside the canal, off the A4091 at Drayton Manor bridge. Formerly the house of Sir Robert Peel. 15 acres of wood and parkland with monkeys, birds, lions, pumas, llamas, sea lions and bears. Daily milking demonstration. *Open daily, Sun only in winter.*

Coventry Canal (see p. 37)

RSWP
Fazeley Junction   Fazeley
P

Drayton
Bassett

N

Bodymoor
Heath

Curdworth 11 Locks
76' 4"

Curd
worth

Min
worth
P

Minworth 3 Locks
16' 8"
S   Tyburn

P

For BCN see
p. 28

Salford
Junction   **Birmingham**

Fazeley
Staffs. Pop 4000. EC Wed. PO, tel, stores, garage. Important only as a road and canal junction, it is a small industrial centre. From the canal it appears more attractive than it really is; useful for supplies.

Fazeley Junction
Staffs. The Birmingham and Fazeley Canal joins the Coventry which comes in from the east. Originally the Coventry was to continue westwards to meet the Trent and Mersey at Fradley; however the Coventry company ran out of money at Fazeley, so the Birmingham and Fazeley continued on to Whittington. The Trent & Mersey company then built a linking arm from Fradley to Whittington, which was later bought by the Coventry company, thus becoming a detached section of their canal.

PUBS & RESTAURANTS
🍺 **Tyburn House** Chester road bridge (just above top lock). Canalside.

🍺 **Hare & Hound** Minworth. Canalside, by Cottage lane bridge. Food.

🍺 **Boat** Minworth. Canalside, by Caters bridge.

🍺 ✕ **Beehive** Curdworth. Food, garden.

🍺 **White Horse** Curdworth. Food.

🍺 **Dog & Doublet** Bodymoor Heath. Canalside.

🍺 **Plough & Hare** Watling st, Fazeley. Food.

🍺 **Three Tuns Inn** (Tamworth 62329) 100yds W of junction. Overnight moorings for customers. W Food.

Drayton Bassett, Birmingham & Fazeley Canal. *Derek Pratt.*

Coventry Canal

This was one of the most consistently profitable canals ever built in Britain. Construction started in 1768 with two main objectives: the first, to connect Coventry with the Bedworth coalfields was quickly achieved and traffic was flowing in 1769; the second, to connect Coventry with the Trent & Mersey was not fulfilled until 1790. Even then, the canal was 12 miles short of its intended terminus at Fradley and the line was already being completed by the Birmingham & Fazeley to Whittington Brook and thence to Fradley by the Trent & Mersey. This latter section was subsequently purchased by the Coventry, resulting in the now detached portion of the Coventry from Whittington Brook to Fradley.

With the completion of the Oxford Canal in 1790 and the Grand Junction in 1805 profits rose, and the traffic from other adjoining canals – the Ashby, Wyrley & Essington and Trent & Mersey all contributed to this prosperity.

Although not a beautiful canal, it has surprises enough for the navigator and walker.

Maximum dimensions
Length: 72'
Beam: 7'
Headroom: 6' 6"
COVENTRY Basin to
HAWKESBURY JUNCTION (Oxford Canal): 5½ miles, no locks
MARSTON JUNCTION (Ashby Canal): 8¼ miles, no locks
Boot Wharf, Nuneaton: 10½ miles, no locks
Hartshill: 14 miles, no locks
Atherstone Top Lock: 16½ miles, no locks
Polesworth: 21½ miles, 11 locks
Glascote Bottom Lock: 25½ miles, 13 locks
FAZELEY JUNCTION (Birmingham & Fazeley Canal): 27 miles, 13 locks
Whittington Brook: 32½ miles, 13 locks
Huddlesford Junction: 34 miles, 13 locks
FRADLEY JUNCTION (Trent & Mersey Canal): 38 miles, 13 locks

11½ miles

The canal begins at a large 'Y' shaped basin overlooked by tall new buildings and attractive old canal warehouses. Its course to Hawkesbury Junction is narrow, winding and flanked mostly by buildings, although the water is surprisingly clear. Alongside the navigation between Longford Bridge and Hawkesbury Junction, is the course taken by the Oxford Canal prior to 1836 Only the Hawkesbury Colliery Farm provides a focal point in the industrial wasteland before the canal passes the housing estates of Bedworth in a long cutting. At Marston Junction the Ashby Canal branches east After passing the disused Griff Colliery Arm to the west, the navigation skirts Nuneaton through a succession of housing estates and allotments

Hawkesbury Junction
Also known as Sutton Stop, after the name of the first lock keeper. It is a busy canal centre, with plenty of retired narrow boats permanently moored there. Recently restored, the Junction received an award from the Business and Industry Panel for the Environment. It also has a real old canal pub, a stop lock (still functioning) and a derelict pumping house, which used to pump water up into the canal from a well. Its 'Newcomentype' atmospheric steam engine was installed in 1821, having already completed nearly 100 years service at the nearby Griff Colliery.

Coventry
West Midlands. Pop 330,000. EC Thur, MD Wed/Fri/Sat. All services. The town was largely destroyed during the Second World War and consequently today is a modern and well-planned city. The motor car industry thrives.

Herbert Art Gallery & Museum Jordan Well. Local art, natural history, archaeology, industry. Open daily (Sun 14.00-17.00).
Coventry Cathedral Designed by Sir Basil Spence and completed in 1962. The modern stained-glass windows all reflect their light towards the altar, behind which is the tapestry by Graham Sutherland. The font, a boulder from a hillside near Bethlehem, stands in front of the Baptistry window by John Piper.
Cathedral Church of St Michael Only the ruins of the old cathedral destroyed by

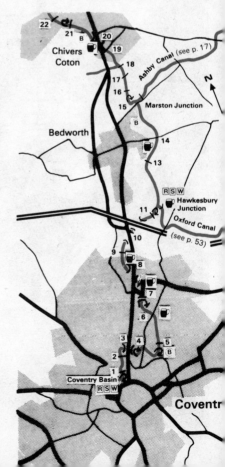

the Luftwaffe in 1940 still remain. From the battlements of the 300ft tower and spire a splendid view of the city can be obtained.

St John's Church Built in 14thC and used as a prison when the Scots were defeated by Oliver Cromwell. From the incident comes the phrase 'sent to Coventry'.

Bedworth
Warwicks. Pop 32,500. EC Wed. MD Tue/ Fri/Sat. A mining town, church by Bodley and Garner 1888–90. almshouses 1840.

Chilvers Coton
Warwicks. A suburb of Nuneaton. Its church dates from 1946 and was built by German prisoners of war.

Nuneaton
Warwicks. Pop 63,980. EC Thur. MD Sat. All services. Midlands town with much industrial development. On the derelict Griff Colliery canal arm are the hollows said to be the origin of the Red Deeps of the 'Mill on the Floss' by George Elliot, who was born here in 1819.

Nuneaton Museum and Art Gallery
Riversley Park. Archaeology. Geological and mining relics. Ethnography. Personalia collection of the novelist George Elliot. *Open daily.*

Arbury Hall 2m SW of canal off B4102. Originally an Elizabethan house, gothicized 1750-1800. Fine pictures, furniture, china and glass. The Hall is in a beautiful park setting. *Open Easter-Oct.*

BOATYARDS & BWB

Ⓑ **Club Line Cruisers** Swan Lane Wharf, Coventry (58864). Ⓡ Ⓢ Ⓦ Ⓓ Pump-out. Boat hire, slipway, gas, dry dock, boat building and repair, mooring, toilets, showers, winter storage.

Ⓑ **Gilbert Bros.** Charity Dock, Furnace rd. Bedworth (313122). Ⓓ Moorings. repairs (including boatbuilding), dry dock, chandlery, toilets.

Ⓑ **Nautocraft Marina** Boot Wharf (Br 20), Nuneaton (5833). Ⓢ Ⓦ Ⓓ Pump-out (*Mon–Fri*). Boat hire, slipway, boat building and repair, mooring, chandlery, toilets.

PUBS & RESTAURANTS

✕ ❢ **Hotel Leofric** Broadgate, Coventry (21371). Food, reductions for children.

🍺 **Navigation** Canalside, at bridge 6.

🍺 **Royal Hotel** near bridge 7.

🍺 **New Inn** Canalside at bridge 8.

🍺 **Greyhound** Hawkesbury Junction. Canalside. An authentic canal pub.

🍺 **Navigation** Bedworth. Canalside, at bridge 14.

🍺 ✕ **Engine Inn & Royal Scot Grill** Kings st, Bedworth (4316). Food, reductions for children.

🍺 **Boot** Boot wharf, Nuneaton. Canalside. Food.

🍺 **Old Wharf Inn** Wharf Inn bridge, Nuneaton. Canalside. Food.

Hartshill, Coventry Canal. *Derek Pratt.*

Coventry

Atherstone

15½ miles (Nuneaton to Fazeley)

Leaving Nuneaton, the canal passes through a curiously exciting landscape of quarries and spoil heaps, with unexpected views of open countryside across the Anker valley. The water here has a distinct rust colour. Passing Atherstone, the canal descends the narrow locks to converge with the River Anker through arable land. Approaching the next industrial belt, the skyline is a romantic 18thC vision of industry. The navigation leaves the suburban housing for lightly wooded fields and open country after meeting the Birmingham & Fazeley Canal at Fazeley Junction.

Hartshill
Warwicks. PO, tel, stores, garage. A Nuneaton suburb with extraordinary man-made surroundings—a landscape of canyons, pits, mountains, all of bright red earth sharp against the sky.
Mancetter
Warwicks. PO, tel, stores, garage. 13thC church with 18thC slate tombstones with Georgian incised lettering. Almshouses with pretty Victorian Gothic details.
Atherstone
Warwicks. Pop 5450. EC Thur. MD Tue/ Fri. PO, tel, stores, garage, station, cinema. A pleasant town with a strong 18thC feeling. On Shrove Tuesday hundreds of people play medieval football in the streets. Set high among trees to the west is Merevale Hall, an early 19thC Tudor mansion. Also to the west are the remains of the 12thC abbey and 13thC church.
Grendon
Warwicks. A small church set in beautiful parkland.
Polesworth
Warwicks. Pop 4240. EC Wed. PO, tel, stores, garage, station. The splendid gatehouse and celestory are all that remain of the 10thC abbey. Calor gas end supplies available at bridge 53.
Alvecote
Warwicks. PO, tel, stores. A mining village surrounded by the remains of industrialisation. The church has a weatherboarded bellcote and surviving Norman work inside.
Amington
Staffs. PO, tel, stores, garage. The church, built by Street 1864, has a Burne-Jones stained glass window.
Tamworth
Staffs. Pop 34,000. EC Wed. MD Sat. All services. Originally a Saxon town, it is built predominantly of grey-black stone. The castle is of Norman origin but dates mostly from the time of Henry VIII. Town Hall by Sir Thomas Guy, founder of Guy's Hospital. St Editha's church contains monuments and stained glass by William Morris. The Castle Museum has coins from the Tamworth Mint of Saxon and Norman periods and items of local interest.

BOATYARDS & BWB

Ⓑ **BWB Hartshill Yard** Clock Hill, Hartshill. (Chapel End 392250). Ⓦ (Ⓓ emergency only). Dry dock.

Ⓑ **Valley Cruisers** Atherstone (3016). ⓇⓌⒹ Pump-out. Boat hire and boat-building, slipway, gas, repairs, mooring, toilets. *Closed Nov–Feb.*

Ⓑ **BWB Fazeley Yard** 200 yards west of the junction. ⓇⓌ Slipway, moorings. Hire small craft.

PUBS

🍺 **White Horse** Nuneaton, near bridge 23.
🍺 **Anchor** Hartshill. By bridge 29. Canal-side. Food.
🍺 **Plough** Mancetter. Food.
🍺 **Kings Head** Atherstone. By A5 bridge. Canalside. Food.
🍺 **Royal Oak** Polesworth. Food.
🍺 **Gate Inn** Amington. Canalside. Food, PO box, tel.
🍺 **Anchor** Anchor Bridge, Glascote. Canalside. Food.
🍺 **Red Lion** Hopwas. Canalside. Food.
🍺✗ **Chequers Inn** Hopwas. (Tamworth 2429). Canalside. Food.

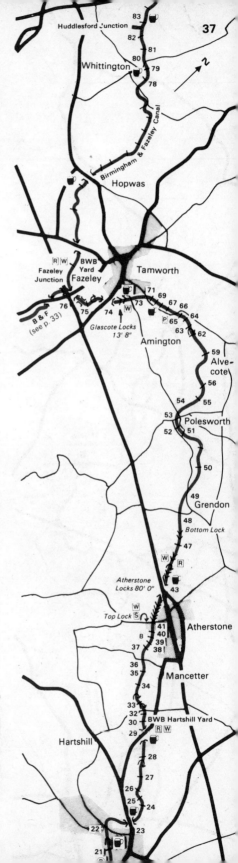

Fradley

11 miles (Fazeley to Fradley)

From Fazeley to Whittington is theoretically the Birmingham & Fazeley Canal, from Whittington to Fradley is a disjointed section of the Coventry all due to a Coventry Canal Company cash crisis at the time of construction. The bridges between numbers 77 and 78 are current evidence of this anomaly.

Following the course of the River Tame below Hopwas, there is a delightful wooded stretch through the Whittington firing ranges (no landing), then a side cut embankment with a view of Tamworth. It is then flat open country to the junction with the Trent & Mersey at Fradley

Hopwas
Staffs. EC Wed. PO, tel, stores. Set among trees above the village is the church an unusual 20thC Arts and Crafts design. To the north is Hopwas Wood; anyone walking should look out for the danger flags of Whittington firing ranges.

Whittington
Staffs. PO, tel, stores, garage. The village centre is attractive. Large 19thC church with conspicuous spire.

Huddlesford
Staffs. PO box. A well named hamlet cut in half by the railway line. At Huddlesford Junction the Wyrley & Essington Canal used to join the Coventry, but this part has long been abandoned.

Lichfield
Staffs. PO, tel, stores, garage, cinema, station. The town has a long history, its earliest charter being granted in 1387. The huge brown stone cathedral, built in 1195-1325, is unique in that it has retained its three spires. The west front has over 100 carved figures, many restored in the 19thC. The streets close by the cathedral and leading to the market square are the oldest dating from the Tudor period. A fine 17thC house in the market square is the birthplace of Dr Johnson, now a museum. Associations with Erasmus Darwin, founder of the Lunar Society. Local history and art exhibitions in the Norman castle art gallery and museum in Bird st.

Fradley
Staffs. PO, tel, stores. A small village that owed its prosperity to a now disused airfield.

Fradley Junction
Staffs. PO box, tel, garage. A well established canal centre marking the northern end of the Coventry Canal.

BOATYARDS & BWB

BWB Fradley Maintenance Yard
Fradley Junction. (Burton on Trent 790236) R S W Toilets.
ⓑ **Swan Line Cruisers** Fradley Junction. (Burton on Trent 790332). W D Moorings, chandlery, boat hire, gas, dry dock, boat building & repairs, provisions. *Closed Sat afternoon and Sun in winter.*
ⓑ **Lichfield Marina** Streethay Basin, Burton road, Streethay, Lichfield, Staffs (Lichfield 51981) R S W Moorings, slipway. Boat sales and repairs, outboard engine sales and service. Chandlery. *Closed Tue.*

PUBS

🍺 **Swan** Whittington. Food.
🍺✕ **Dog Inn** Whittington. (252). Food.
🍺✕ **Bell** Main st, Whittington. (377). Food.
🍺 **Plough** Huddlesford Junction. Canalside. Food.
🍺 **Swan** Fradley Junction. Canalside. Food.

Grand Union Canal

The Grand Union comprises at least 8 separate canals, linking London with Birmingham, Leicester and Nottingham. Once owned and operated by separate companies, they made up the spine of southern England's transport system until the advent of the railways.

The original part was the Grand Junction Canal, constructed at the turn of the 18thC to provide a short cut between Brentford and Braunston, cutting 60 miles off the journey from the Midlands to London. Having wide locks and numerous branches to important towns, it soon became busy and popular. If the other companies had followed the Grand Junction's example, and widened their canals, the history of English canals might have turned out very different.

Meanwhile in London, in 1812, the Regent's Canal Company was formed to cut a new canal round London to Limehouse. This proved highly successful and 10 years later the Hertford Union was built for connection with the River Lee.

The Regent's Canal Company later acquired the Grand Junction and others.

The whole system was integrated as the Grand Union Canal Company in 1929, and a massive programme of modernisation was launched in 1932, aided by the Government. Widening locks, piling and dredging work took place but the grant ran out before it was finished. The Grand Union could only decline commercially, but it remains today a vital part of the inland cruising network.

Maximum dimensions
Brentford and Paddington to Birmingham (Camp Hill Top Lock)
Length: 72', Beam: 12' 6"
Headroom: 7' 11"
Norton Junction to Foxton Junction
Length: 72', Beam: 7'
Headroom: 7' 6"
Market Harborough to Leicester
Length: 72', Beam: 10'
Headroom: 7'

Foxton Locks, Leicester Section of the Grand Union. *Derek Pratt.*

Watford

Gayton Junction to Yelvertoft 17 miles

The canal meanders sharply on its way towards Norton Junction where the main line turns west and the attractive Leicester Section continues northwards. Overhanging trees and shallow banks can make it impossible for two boats to pass on the Leicester Section. The 412ft summit level, above the Watford staircase, is maintained for the next 22 miles.

Nether Heyford
Northants. Pop 730. PO, tel, stores.
Weedon
Northants. Pop 1490. EC Thur. PO, tel, stores, garage. The Victorian church has a Norman tower. To the north are the remains of Weedon barracks.
Brockhall
Northants. PO box. Tudor Hall with fine 18thC interiors.
Whilton
Northants. PO, tel, stores. 1m E of canal. The site of Banaventa, a Roman settlement, lies to the west.
Buckby Wharf
Northants. PO box, tel, stores.
Watford
Northants. Pop 230. EC Sat. PO, tel, stores. The 13thC church contains some interesting monuments. Watford Court is partly 17thC with Victorian additions.
Crick
Northants. Pop 780. PO, tel, stores. The large church contains much decorative stonework and a circular font.
Crick Tunnel 1528 yards long. Opened in 1814. Quicksands caused a change of route, greatly affecting work.
Yelvertoft
Northants. Pop 450. PO, tel, stores, garage.
Winwick
Northants. 1m SE bridge 23. A semi-deserted village. Surviving 16thC Manor House with Tudor gateway.

BOATYARDS & BWB

Ⓑ **Concoform Marine** The Boatyard, High st, Weedon. (40739). Ⓡ Ⓢ Ⓦ Ⓟ Ⓓ Pump-out (*Tue–Fri*). Boat hire, gas, mooring, winter storage. *Closed Sun & Mon summer, Sat & Sun winter.*
Ⓑ **Waterways Holidays** Narrow Boat Inn, Stowe Hill, Weedon. (41365). Ⓡ Ⓢ Ⓦ Ⓓ Pump-out. Boat hire, gas, dry dock, boat building & repair, mooring, toilets, provisions. *Closed Sun.*
Ⓑ **Whilton Marine** Whilton locks. (Long Buckby 842577). Ⓡ Ⓢ Ⓦ Ⓟ Ⓓ Moorings, repairs, chandlery, groceries, hire cruisers, slipway, clubhouse. Bar. Short boat trips.
Ⓑ **Weltonfield Narrowboats** Weltonfield Farm, Bridge 2. (Long Buckby 842282). Ⓡ Ⓢ Ⓦ Ⓓ Pump-out (arrange by phone). Boat hire, gas, boat building & repair, toilets, shop, boat lift.

PUBS & RESTAURANTS

🍺 **New Inn** Weedon, near bridge 24.
🍺 ✕ **Crossroads Hotel** Weedon. (354). Food.
🍺 **Narrow Boat** Weedon. (336). Canalside, at bridge 26. Sandwiches and snacks.
🍺 **Stag's Head** Watford Gap. Canalside.
🍺 **New Inn** Canalside, at Buckby Top lock.
🍺 **White Horse** Norton (1½m W of bridge 15).
🍺 ✕ **Red Lion Inn** Main st, Crick. (342). Food, skittles.
🍺 **Wheatsheaf** 15 Main st, Crick. (284).
🍺 **Knightly Arms** High st, Yelvertoft. Food.

Foxton

17 miles

The Leicester Section wanders northwards,
and the Welford Arm, completed in 1814,
branches south east for 1½m, linking the
canal with the Welford and Sulby
reservoirs, and reaches its terminus in a
small basin. The arm derelict for many
years, was re-opened in 1969. The main
line continues to the top of Foxton
Locks, then falls 75 feet to join the 'Old
Union' line to Leicester. At the bottom of
the locks the Market Harborough Arm
branches off and meanders eastwards
towards Market Harborough Basin.

North Kilworth
Leics. Pop 710. PO, tel, stores, garage.
Main road village. Useful supply centre.
Welford
Northants. Pop 710. PO, tel, stores, garage.
The best part is the restored canal wharf.
A public footpath from the village passes
between the 2 reservoirs.
Stanford Hall 2m W of bridge 31. A
William and Mary brick mansion built in
1697-1700. Includes motor-car and
motor-bicycle museum, experimental
flying machine. *Open Thur, Sat, Sun
afternoons, Easter-end Sept, Bank Hols.*
Stanford church contains fine woodwork,
14thC to 16thC stained glass and many
monuments.
Husbands Bosworth
Leics. Pop 730. PO, tel, stores, garage.
There is a good church with a stumpy
spire. Home of an annual steam engine
rally.
Husbands Bosworth Tunnel 1166 yards
long, opened in 1813.
Foxton
Leics. Pop 360. EC Sat. PO, tel, stores.
The church contains a Norman font.
Foxton Locks The Foxton staircase, opened
in 1812. Two staircases of 5 locks each
with a passing pound in the middle. The
locks work on the sidepond principle, and
remain today as when first built.
Foxton Inclined Plane
Opened in 1900 to bypass Foxton Locks,
closed 1911, only the ruins remain. It
worked on the counter balance system, 2
caissons carrying 2 narrow boats or 1 barge
moving sideways on rails up and down the
plane. A steam driven winch pulling an
endless cable was used to start the caissons
moving. The journey time was reduced
from seventy to twelve minutes. Mechanical
problems and high running costs, plus the
fact that the planned widening of the
Watford flight never took place, soon made
the plane a white elephant.
Market Harborough
*Leics. Pop 14,000. EC Wed. MD Tue/Sat.
PO, tel, stores, garage, banks, station.*
Established as a market town by 1203.
The pleasure of the town centre is weakened
by the presence of the A6.
**Archaeological & Historical Society
Museum** County Library, The Square.
Contains the society's own collection and
illustrates local life from the earliest times.
Relics of the Battle of Naseby.
Parish Church of St Dionysius High st.
Built in the 14thC by Scropes and enlarged
a century later. The broach spire and west
tower are notable. Fine window tracery.
Old Grammar School High st. Founded
by Robert Smyth who was born here. It
stands on wooden carved pillars, and behind
the arches was held the ancient butter
market.

BOATYARDS & BWB
Ⓑ **North Kilworth Narrow Boats**
Kilworth Marina, Lutterworth, Leics.
880484). Ⓡ Ⓢ Ⓦ Ⓓ Pump-out. Boat
hire, slipway, gas, boat building & repair,
mooring, chandlery, toilets, provisions,
winter storage, off-licence.
Ⓑ **Black Prince Narrow Boats** Canal
wharf, Lower Welford. (881519).
Ⓡ Ⓢ Ⓦ Ⓓ Pump-out. Boat hire, gas,
boat building & repair, mooring, chandlery,
toilets, provisions.

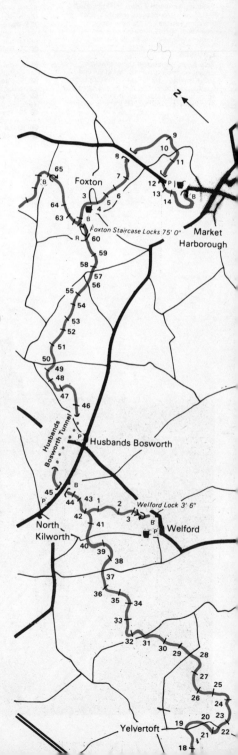

Ⓑ **Anglo-Welsh Narrow Boats;
Harborough Marine Ltd** The Canal Basin,
Leicester rd, Market Harborough. (6/076).
Ⓡ Ⓢ Ⓦ Ⓟ Ⓓ   Pump-out (*Mon–Fri*). Boat
hire, slipway, gas, dry dock, boat building &
repair, mooring, chandlery, toilets.

Ⓑ **Foxton Boat Services** Bottom Lock,
Foxton, (Kibworth 2285). Ⓡ Ⓢ Ⓦ Ⓟ Ⓓ
Pump-out. Boat hire, slipway, gas, boat
building, repairs (24 hrs), mooring,
chandlery, toilets, showers, provisions,
winter storage, cafe, restaurant, bar.

CRUISES

Trip boat Vagabond Canal trips for
casual visitors on summer Sundays and
Bank Holidays, from Foxton Bottom Lock;
available for charter by parties any other day
(minimum 20 passengers, maximum 51).
Telephone Kibworth 2285 for information.

PUBS & RESTAURANTS

🍺 **Swan** North Kilworth. (Kilworth 2464).
✕❢ **Elizabethan Restaurant** High st,
Welford. (311).
🍺 **Shoulder of Mutton** High st, Welford.
(375).
✕❢ **Wharf House Hotel** Welford. (238).
At the end of the Welford Arm. B&B.
Dinner on Thur, Fri & Sat.
✕❢ **Fernie Lodge** Berridge lane,
Husbands Bosworth. (551). Good food,
must book. *Closed Sun.*
🍺 ✕ **Bell** High st, Husbands Bosworth.
Food.
🍺 **Angel Hotel** High st, Market
Harborough. (3125). Food.
🍺 ✕ **Peacock Inn** The Square, Market
Harborough. (2269). Good English food.
🍺 **Six Packs** Leicester rd, Market
Harborough. (2153). Food.
🍺 ✕ **Three Swans Hotel** High st, Market
Harborough. Food.
🍺 **Black Horse** Foxton. Canalside. Food.
🍺 **Shoulder of Mutton** Main st, Foxton.

Foxton inclined plane in its heyday.

(see p. 58)

Leicester

15 miles

From Foxton the canal continues in a generally northerly direction towards Leicester, remaining quiet and remote. Occasional cuttings and clear water make the canal very river-like. Near Fleckney, locks begin the descent to Leicester. The first views of housing estates and factories are seen at Kilby Bridge, and by South Wigston the town seems to take over. After swinging wide round Glen Parva, the canal follows the River Soar into Leicester and enters the city along a pleasant cutting. A fine canalside walk leads into the city centre by West Bridge. The entry to Leicester is outstanding among large towns.

Navigational note

The Grand Union Canal's Leicester section does *not* terminate at Leicester: boats can continue straight through down to the Trent near Nottingham (25 miles and 18 locks away to the north). North of Kings lock (38) the navigation is actually the canalised river Soar all the way down to the Trent. From Leicester to the Trent is covered on pages 58 & 59 of this book. Limiting dimensions of this waterway are approximately the same as for the section between Leicester and Market Harborough, i.e. the locks are 14ft wide, but the cross-section of some bridges prohibits the use of 14ft-beam boats. For details ring BWB at Watford 26422 or Leicester 882795.

Gumley
Leics. ½m W bridge 63. PO box, tel. Gumley Hall has an Italianate tower.
Smeeton Westerby
Leics. EC Wed. PO, tel, stores. The church is Victorian, by Woodyer.
Saddington
Leics. EC Sat. PO, tel, stores.
Saddington Tunnel
880 yards long, completed in 1797, after great difficulties, being built crooked. Interesting bat population.
Fleckney
Leics. Pop 1800. EC Wed. PO, tel, stores, garage. An industrial village, surrounded by open fields.
Wistow
Leics. A church and a Hall. The church with Norman work is mostly 18thC. the Hall, Jacobean in principle was largely rebuilt in the 19thC.
Newton Harcourt
Leics. EC Sat. PO, tel, stores. A well-known beauty spot, popular on Sunday afternoons. The church tower is 13thC, the rest Victorian. The 17thC Hall has a fine gateway.
Kilby Bridge
Leics. PO, tel, garage (24hr).
Wigston
Leics. PO, tel, stores, garage. Now part of Leicester. The handsome church dates from the 14thC. The cottages in Spa lane, with their long strips of upper window indicate an old Leicester industry, stocking making. Tiny Norman church at Wigston Parva and a monument to the Roman town of Veronae.
Blaby
Leics. Pop 2010. PO, tel, stores, garage. The church is partly 14thC, with a fine 18thC gallery.
Leicester
Leics. Pop 282,000. EC Mon. MD Wed/Fri/ Sat. All services. Roman remains appear conspicuously. Leicester cathedral was originally Norman, though much re-building was done by Bodley, Street and Brandon. Leicester is also famous for its cheese.
Leicester Museum & Art Gallery New walk. (26832). 18thC and 19thC English paintings and water-colours. Also modern and German Expressionist paintings. Ceramics gallery. Archives and geology.
Newarke Houses Museum The Newarke (50988). Social history of the locality from 1500 to the present day. Locally made

clocks and a clockmaker's workshop. Also shows the history of the hosiery, costume and lace industries.

Museum of Technology Corporation Rd (61330). Development of power and transport in hosiery industry.

Museum of Costume Wygstone House, St Nicholas Circle. 18thC-20thC costumes.

Belgrave Hall Thurmaston rd. (61610). Small Queen Anne house and garden. Early 18thC and 19thC furniture. Also stables, coaches and agricultural collection.

Jewry Wall & Museum of Archaeology Great Central st. (22392). Leicester was once a Roman capital named Ratae Coritanorum. The Jewry Wall, a small portion of which remains, may have been part of a basilica or baths. Two Roman pavements, patterned mosaics, can be seen in situ.

Raw Dykes Aylestone rd. Between the gasworks and the electricity station. A fragment of Roman aqueduct remains.

Leicester Abbey All that remains is a mansion built from the ruins and the old stone wall surrounding the grounds. Wolsey was buried here in 1530.

Guildhall Guildhall lane. (21523). Contains fine oak panelling and a massive carved chimney-piece dated 1637.

Clock Tower A Victorian commemoration to four of Leicester's benefactors: Simon de Montfort, Alderman Gabriel Newton, William Wyggeston and Sir Thomas White.

Information Bureau Bishop st. (Leicester 20644). ½m E of bridge 1 (near cathedral). Pamphlets and information on the town.

Aylestone
Leics. PO, tel, stores, garage. A Leicester suburb, east of the canal. The church contains an interesting 1930 stained glass window. West of the canal, the Soar is crossed by an old stone packhorse bridge of 8 arches, possibly 15thC.

Glen Parva
Leics. PO, tel, stores, garage. Suburb of Leicester. 6thC grave ornaments have been excavated from a Saxon cemetery.

BOATYARDS & BWB

Ⓑ **Ian Goode Narrow Boats** Debdale Wharf, Kibworth. (3034). Ⓡ Ⓦ Ⓓ Pump-out (*Mar–Nov*). Boat hire, gas, boat & engine repairs, mooring, winter storage. *Closed winter weekends.*

Ⓑ **BWB Kilby Bridge Yard** Kilby Bridge. (Leicester 882795). Ⓡ Ⓢ Ⓦ

Ⓑ **Blaby Marine Centre** Wharf Way, Glen Parva, Leicester (Wigston 778899). Ⓡ Ⓢ Ⓦ Slipway, boat building & repair, mooring, chandlery, toilets, winter storage. *Closed Tue.*

Ⓑ **Leicester Marina** Old Bridge, Thurcaston, Leicester. (357575). Ⓡ Ⓦ Ⓓ Pump-out. Slipway, gas, boat building, mooring, chandlery, winter storage, 55 seater day trip boat for charter.

PUBS & RESTAURANTS

🍺 **Queens Head** Saddington.
🍺 **Kings Head** Smeeton Westerby, Leicester.
🍺 **Bell** Gumley.
Several pubs in Fleckney, unfortunately none in Newton Harcourt.
🍺 **County Arms** Blaby.
🍺 **Black Horse** Blaby.
🍺 **George** Blaby.
🍺 **Navigation** Kilby Bridge.
✕🍷 **Abbey Motor Hotel** Abbey st, Leicester. (50666). Restaurant (except Sun).
🍺 **Ye Olde Bowling Green** Oxford st, Leicester. (24763). Food.
✕🍷 **Barge Buttery** The Post House, Braunstone lane east, Aylestone. (Leicester 51321). Restaurant about 1 mile east of bridge 106.
✕🍷 **Giorgio's** 77 Narborough rd, Leicester. (29267). Formerly La Gioconda. *Closed Sun; Sat L.*
✕ **Good Earth** 19 Belvoir st, Leicester. (58584). Self-service vegetarian restaurant. Lunch only. *Closed Sun.*
✕🍷 **Acropolis** 270 Loughborough rd (A6). (Leicester 63106). Greek and Cypriot. *Closed Sun; Sat L.* Must book.

Near Saddington, Grand Union Leicester Section. *Derek Pratt.*

Braunston

18 miles

From Norton Junction the canal runs
westwards towards Braunston, a big canal
centre. A large boatyard situated on an
arm to the south meets every boating
need. The arm was part of the old route
to Oxford before it was shortened by
building a large embankment (Braunston
Puddle Bank) across the Leam valley to
Braunston Turn. Leaving Braunston, the
Grand Union joins the Oxford Canal to
Napton Junction, a pleasant lock-free
stretch. At Calcutt Locks the descent
towards Warwick begins, passing the
Stockton industrial belt.

Welton
Northants. PO, tel, stores.

Braunston
*Northants. Pop 1190. PO, tel, stores,
launderette.* The village is a well known
canal centre. A fine selection of old
buildings line the canal. The shop by the
bottom lock is full of all sorts of canal relics
and ephemera.

Braunston Tunnel 2042 yards long,
opened in 1796, its construction was
hindered by quicksands. *Two boats of 7ft
beam can pass in this tunnel, but wide
beam boats must get permission from the
lock-keepers at Buckby (Long Buckby 234)
or Braunston (Rugby 890259) to enter
the tunnel. They will then give a clear
passage.*

Lower Shuckburgh
Warwicks. Pop 70. Post box. The church,
built 1846, contains much contrasting
brickwork.

Stockton
Warwicks. EC Sat. PO, tel, stores, garage.
The church is built of Blue Lias, quarried
near Stockton Locks.

Long Itchington
Warwicks. Pop 1680. PO, tel, stores, garage.
Attractive village with 17thC and 18thC
houses and a largely 13thC church.

BOATYARDS & BWB

🅱 **Ladyline/Braunstone Marina**
Braunston. (Rugby 890325).
Ⓡ Ⓢ Ⓦ Ⓟ Ⓓ Moorings, repairs,
chandlery, dry dock, slipway, hire, food,
toilets, showers, gas.

🅱 **Calcutt Boats** Calcutt Top Lock
Stockton, Rugby. (Southam 3757).
Ⓢ Ⓦ Ⓓ Pump-out. Boat hire, slipway,
gas, dry dock, boat building and repairs,
mooring, chandlery, toilets, provisions.
Charter and hotel boats.

PUBS & RESTAURANTS

🍺 **Admiral Nelson** Little Braunston.
Canalside, at lock 3. Canals decor of prints
and lace plates. Food, skittles.

🍺 **White Horse** Welton. Food, skittles.

🍺 **New Inn** Buckby Top Lock. Canalside.

🍺✖ **The Boatman** Braunston.
(Rugby 890313). Popular canalside pub
at Braunston Turn. Bar snacks; garden
with swings. Meals every day except Sun
evening and all day Mon.

🍺 **The Old Plough** Braunston. Food.

🍺 **Two Boats Inn** Long Itchington. Bridge
25.

🍺 **Blue Lias** Stockton. (Southam 2249).
Canalside, at bridge 23. Food, fine selection
of malt whiskies. Animals in garden.

🍺 **Boat** Birdingbury wharf. Canalside, at
bridge 21. Food.

🍺✖ **Cuttle Inn** Long Itchington. Canalside. Petrol adjacent.

Plenty of pubs in Long Itchington village.

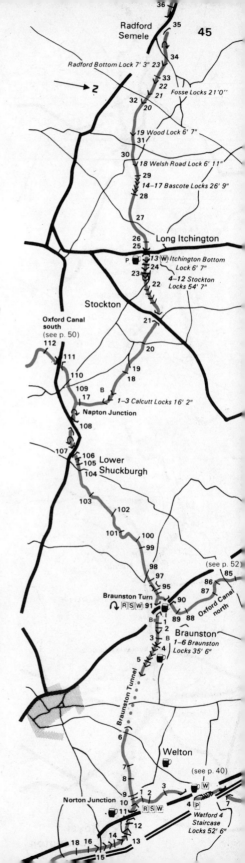

45
Oxford Canal south (see p. 50)
(see p. 52)
Oxford Canal north
(see p. 40)

Radford Semele
Radford Bottom Lock 7' 3" 23
Fosse Locks 21 0''
19 Wood Lock 6' 7"
18 Welsh Road Lock 6' 11"
14–17 Bascote Locks 26' 9"
Long Itchington
13 Ⓦ Itchington Bottom Lock 6' 7"
4–12 Stockton Locks 54' 7"
Stockton
1–3 Calcutt Locks 16' 2"
Napton Junction
Lower Shuckburgh
Braunston Turn Ⓡ Ⓢ Ⓦ
Braunston
1–6 Braunston Locks 35' 6"
Braunston Tunnel
Welton
Norton Junction
Ⓡ Ⓢ Ⓦ
Watford 4 Staircase Locks 52' 6"

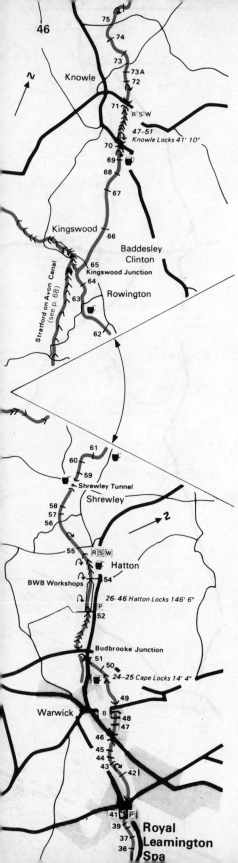

Royal Leamington Spa

16 miles

From Fosse Locks the canal continues west
straight through Leamington, then swings
north west towards Warwick which is best
approached from bridge 46. As the canal
skirts round the town to Budbrooke
Junction, where the old Warwick and
Napton Canal joined the Warwick and
Birmingham; the arm leading into Warwick
is now disused. West of Budbrooke
Junction is the first of the 21 daunting
Hatton Locks. At Kingswood is the
junction with the Stratford-upon-Avon
Canal, restored by volunteers in 1964,
and now owned by the National Trust. The
Stratford-on-Avon Canal Manager's
office at Kingswood Junction (Lapworth
3370) will give information on the canal.
After Kingswood, the canal moves north
towards Solihull. The remains of the old
locks can be seen alongside the
new, together with the sideponds. These
are the northernmost wide locks for many
miles.

Radford Semele
Warwicks. Pop 1270. EC Thur. PO, tel,
stores, garage. Suburb of Leamington.
Radford Hall is a reconstructed
Jacobean building. The church is
Victorian.

Offchurch
Warwicks. PO, tel, stores, garage.
Residential village. The church with its
tall grey stone tower contains some
Norman work. To the west lies Offchurch
Bury, originally a 17thC house, now with
a Gothic facade

Royal Leamington Spa
Warwicks. Pop 44,970. EC Mon/Thur. All
services. A largely mid-Victorian spa
town. J. Cundall, a local architect of
some note designed several buildings
including the town hall. Since the
Victorian era much industrialisation
has taken place.

Art Gallery & Museum Avenue rd.
British, Dutch and Flemish paintings of the
16thC and 17thC. Also modern art,
pottery, porcelain and 18thC English
drinking glasses. Victorian costume and
objects. *Open daily.*

All Saints' Church Bath st. Begun in 184
to the design of J. C. Jackson, the church
of Gothic style, not always correct in deta
The north transept has a rose window
patterned on Rouen Cathedral; the west
window is by Kempe.

Jephson Gardens Alongside Newbold
terrace, north of bridge 40. Beautiful ornamental gardens named after Dr Jephson
(1798-1878), the local practitioner who wa
largely responsible for the spa's high
medical reputation.

Information Bureau Royal Pump Room
Dormer place. (21215).

Warwick
Warwicks. Pop 18,690. EC Thur. MD Wed
Sat. All services. Historic town which still
contains many medieval buildings.

Church of St Mary's Of Norman origin,
it contains a large 12thC crypt. Much of
the building was burnt down in 1694. The
rebuilt church has a pseudo-Gothic tower

Warwick County Museum Market plac
Mainly local interest. Includes the Sheldor
tapestry map of Warwickshire which dates
from 1588. *Open daily, closed Fri; Sun*
winter.

Doll Museum Oken's House, Castle st.
Open daily.

Court House Jury st. The present buildin
which dates from 1725, was built on the
site of a 16thC civic building.

Lord Leycester Hospital High st. The
hospital was founded by the Earl of
Leycester in 1571. It is now a hospital for
retired or disabled Servicemen.

Warwick Castle Castle Hill. The exterior
is a famous example of a 14thC fortificatio
Inside are pictures by Rubens, Van Dyck
and Velasquez. Capability Brown
grounds. *Open Good Fri-mid Sept daily.*

Hatton
Warwicks. Scattered around the top of the Hatton locks. The church is partly perpendicular, partly Victorian. North of Hatton is Hasely. Its small church still retains box pews and dates from the 13thC.

Shrewley
Warwicks. PO, tel, stores, garage. Useful source of supplies.

Shrewley Tunnel 433 yards long, opened in 1799 with the completion of the Warwick and Birmingham Canal. It is remarkable for the very clearly defined path over the top of the tunnel which a towing horse would use while its boat was 'legged' through the tunnel. This horsepath in fact goes through its own miniature tunnel for 40 yards and emerges at the north west end above and beside the canal tunnel.
This tunnel allows two 7ft boats to pass; keep to the right.

Rowington
Warwicks. Pop 790. PO, tel, stores. Some 17thC and 18thC buildings. The 13thC church by the canal has a fine peal of bells.

Wroxall
Warwicks. 1½m NE of Rowington. Remains of Benedictine Abbey founded in c.1135. Its church with a 14thC nave and 17thC tower survives. A gloomy Victorian mansion replaced a Tudor house bought by Sir Christopher Wren for his son in 1713.

Kingswood
Warwicks. All services. The village is scattered over a wide area from the Grand Union to the Stratford-on-Avon Canal. The centre is 1m to the west, around the ambitious 15thC church. The main feature of interest is the canal junction. Note particularly the iron turnover bridge by the lock at the junction which is split to allow the towing rope to pass through without being unhitched from the horse. Such bridges are a feature of the Stratford-on-Avon Canal.

Packwood House
Hockley Heath. 2m W of bridge 66. (Lapworth 2024). Timber-framed Tudor house, enlarged in the 17thC. Tapestry, needlework and furniture. The 17thC yew garden was laid out to represent the Sermon on the Mount, the trees taking the place of Jesus and his followers. *Open afternoons. Apr-Sept, closed Mon, Fri. Oct-Mar, open Wed, Sat, Sun, Bank Hols.* National Trust property.

BOATYARDS & BWB
ⓑ **BWB Hatton Workshops** Canal la, Hatton, Warwick – near the top Hatton Locks. (42192). Ⓢ Ⓦ Dry dock available for hire, also crane for boats up to 2 tons.
ⓑ **Boats (Warwick)** Nelson lane, Warwick. (42968). Ⓢ Ⓦ Ⓓ Pump-out. Boat hire, gas, chandlery, toilets. *Closed Sun.*

PUBS & RESTAURANTS
✖ **Moore's Cafe** 41 The Parade, Leamington Spa. Food. *Closed Sun.*
✖❢ **Il Portico** 50 Clarendon st, Leamington Spa. (24471). Italian food. *Closed Sun.*
🍺 **Stag Inn** Offchurch. Food.
🍺 ✖ **White Lion Inn** Radford Semele. (Leamington Spa 25770/20230). Food *(except Sun).* Coaching inn, built in 1622. Garden.
✖❢ **Aylesford Restaurant** 1 High st, Warwick. (42799). Extensive menu. *(Closed Sun.)*
🍺 ✖ **New Inn** Hatton. (Warwick 42427). Lunches & dinners *(except Sun).*
🍺 **Cape of Good Hope** Cape Locks, Warwick. Canalside. Food.
🍺 ✖ **Lord Leycester Hotel** Jury st, Warwick. (41481). Restaurant.
🍺 ✖ **Westgate Arms** Bowling Green st, Warwick. (42362).
🍺 **Navigation** Kingswood. Canalside. Food.
🍺 **Ye Olde New Inn** Turners green, Rowington. Canalside. Food.
🍺 **Cockhorse Inn** Rowington. Food.
🍺 **Durham Ox** Shrewley. Food.
✖❢ **Chadwick Manor Hotel** Knowle. (2821). Food, residential.

✖ **Coffee Pot** 2 Station rd, Knowle. (5554). Food. *EC Thur. Closed Sun.*
🍺 **Black Boy** Knowle, Canalside, at bridge 69. Food.
✖❢ **Florentine** 15 Kenilworth rd, Knowle. (6449). Italian cooking. *Closed Sun; Mon L; B. Hols.*

Grand Union main line

Birmingham

5 miles

Continuing north west, the canal passes through Birmingham's expanding suburbia. Supplies are available in plenty, but the embankment makes access rather difficult. Beyond Olton Bridge, housing estates and disused wharves accompany the canal, and boatmen should be wary of rubbish in the water. Access to and from the canal becomes increasingly difficult. Camp Hill Locks and all the succeeding locks are narrow only boats of 7ft beam or less can pass. The former Birmingham and Warwick Junction Canal runs north from Bordesley Junction to join the Birmingham and Fazeley and Tame Valley Canals at Salford Junction. It was opened in 1844 to by-pass the heavily locked stretches of the B & F at Ashted and Aston. The five Garrison Locks carry the canal down to the Erdington level where there is a stop lock.
Birmingham and its canal navigations are described in full on pages 23–31 of this book.

Catherine de Barnes
Warwicks. Tel, stores, garage. A convenient supply centre with easy access from the canal.

Solihull
West Midlands. Pop 110,000. EC Wed. All services. A modern commuter development, with fine public buildings. The church is almost all 14thC. The interior contains work of all periods, 17thC pulpit and communion rail, 19thC stained glass.

Elmdon Heath
West Midlands. EC Thur. PO, tel, stores, garage. Suburb of Solihull. Source of supplies for the athletic. Climb up the embankment by bridge 79.

Tyseley Goods Yard ½m SW of bridge 88. Here the Standard Gauge Steam Trust has a large depot for maintaining, storing and reviving private steam railway engines. *Open to visitors weekends April to October* (there is usually at least one locomotive in steam every Sunday) and on 2 big open days every summer. For details write to the Trust at 24 Harborne rd, Edgbaston, Birmingham 15.

Birmingham
West Midlands. Pop 1,107,200. EC Wed. MD Thur. All services. The Bull Ring, one of the most modern shopping centres in Europe, used to be the village green. Now an industrial and commercial city, Birmingham is famous for such men as John Baskerville, William Murdoch, Joseph Priestly, Matthew Boulton and James Watt.
Assay Office Newhall st. (236 6951). Silverware, coins, tokens and medals. Also the Matthew Boulton collection of correspondence and books. *Open by appointment only.*
Aston Hall Frederick rd. 2m N of city. A Jacobean house built by Sir Thomas Holte in 1618-35. Many of the rooms are furnished in period, and there are impressive friezes and ceilings. *Open daily.*
Avery Historical Museum Soho Foundry (558 1112). Machines, instruments, weights and records illustrating the history of weighing. *By appointment only.*

For BCN see pages 25–26

(see p. 25)

Birmingham

(see p. 78)

W & B Canal

(see p. 33) Salford Junction

B & F Canal

Saltley Canal

64
Nechells
Shallow
Lock 6"
59–63
Garrison Locks 34' 5"

95

Bordesley Junction

R S

52–57 Camp Hill Locks 41' 8"

Sparkbrook 91

90 89

88

Tyseley

87
86 A
86 Acock's Green

Olton 85

84

83

82 Ulverley Green

81

80

79

P

Solihull

78
77
76
75
74

Birmingham (cont)

Barber Institute of Fine Arts The University, Edgbaston. Masterpieces by Bellini, Degas, Courbet, Rubens, Rembrandt, Reynolds Gainsborough and other artists before 1900. *Open Mon-Fri, 1st Sun afternoon of every month during term-time.*

Birmingham City Museum & Art Gallery Congreve st. One of the most important museums outside London, with departments of art, ethnography, archaeology, natural history, science and industry. Fine Old Master paintings and an exceptional collection of Pre-Raphaelites. Famous Pinto collections of by-gones and an unusual number of industrial relics. *For opening times ring Information Bureau (235 3411).*

Cannon Hill Museum Pershore rd. Designed primarily for children. Illustrated leisure time pursuits including bird-watching, bee-keeping, fishing and pets ; Safari hut around which the sounds, sights— and smells of the African Bush are recreated.

Geological Departmental Museum The University, Edgbaston. Includes the Holcroft collection of fossils and the Lapworth collection of grapholites. *Open daily by arrangement.*

Sarehole Mill Colebank rd, Hall Green. An 18thC water powered corn mill, once used by Matthew Boulton for metal working and blade grinding. It is still in working order. *Open daily 14.00-19.00 (Sat 11.00-19.00).*

Farmers Bridge An exciting canalside development at Cambrian wharf (the end of the Birmingham & Fazeley Canal, not shown on the map) in which four sky-scrapers, a new canal pub and a restored 18thC street complete with gaslights are grouped beside a recently restored canal basin. The pub is totally canal orientated, sporting much canal paraphernalia and a bar in genuine floating narrow boat. One of the 18thC houses is a canal shop and information centre. Good mooring.

Cannon Hill Edgbaston. Formal gardens, including a Japanese Garden of Contemplation, tropical and sub-tropical plants, adjacent.

Edgbaston Reservoir A 60-acre lake which feeds the Birmingham Canal; sailing and rowing facilities.

Lickey Hills SW boundary of city. 500 acres of hill and moorland. Pony trekking.

Olton Reservoir Near Olton Station. Feeds the Grand Union Canal and floats a medley of sailing boats.

Information Bureau The Council House, Victoria square, Birmingham 1. (235 3411). Weekly information leaflet available from here and from banks and libraries.

BOATYARDS & BWB

Canal shop & Information Centre (021 236 4844). R S W Pump-out. Chandlery, canal ware and publications. Mooring and facilities at Cambrian Wharf.

PUBS & RESTAURANTS

🍺 **Boat Inn** Catherine de Barnes. Food.

🍺 **Long Boat** Farmers bridge top lock, Kingston row, Birmingham 1. Canalside. Food.

✕🍷 **Gino's** Bull Ring Centre. (643 2966). Restaurant.

✕🍷 **Sandonia Restaurant** 509 Hagley rd Birmingham 17. (429 2622). Restaurant (Cypriot).

✕🍷 **La Capanna** Hurst st, Birmingham. (021-622 2287). Italian restaurant. *Closed Sun.*

✕🍷 **Danish Food Centre** 10 Stephensor Place, Birmingham. (021-643 2837). Meals available all day from breakfast to after-theatre supper. *Closed Sun ; Mon D.*

✕🍷 **Salamis Kebab House** 178 Broad st Edgbaston, Birmingham. (021-643 2997). Friendly Greek restaurant. Dinner only (18.00-24.00). *Closed L ; B. Hols.*

Oxford Canal

Authorised in 1769, this was the first canal linking London to Coventry and the Midlands to bring coal south from the Warwickshire coalfields. James Brindley was appointed engineer, and he designed a winding contour canal 91 miles long to join with the Thames at Oxford, where traffic could continue on to London. Brindley died in 1772, and work was continued under Samuel Simcock who saw the whole route opened to traffic in 1790. Although immediately successful, this was a tortuous route, and when the Grand Junction opened a direct route from Braunston to London in 1805, this drew traffic away from the Oxford Canal. Only the outrageously high tolls charged by the Oxford Canal Company for the use of their $5\frac{1}{2}$ mile stretch between Braunston and Napton protected their position.

However, the Oxford now looked outdated, so between 1829-34 a brave modernisation scheme was undertaken cutting 14 miles from the original 36 between Braunston and Coventry. This had the desired effect and the company remained profitable up to the 20th century.

Today the canal is quiet and sleepy with no trade. It passes through outstanding countryside and unspoilt villages.

Maximum dimensions
Length: 70'
Beam: 7'
Headroom: 7'
Main line
OXFORD (River Thames) to
Thrupp: $6\frac{1}{2}$ miles, 4 locks
Lower Heyford: $14\frac{3}{4}$ miles, 9 locks
Aynho Wharf: $20\frac{1}{4}$ miles, 12 locks
Banbury: $27\frac{1}{4}$ miles, 17 locks
Cropredy: $31\frac{1}{2}$ miles, 20 locks
Fenny Compton Wharf: $37\frac{3}{4}$ miles, 29 locks
Napton Bottom Lock: 47 miles, 38 locks
NAPTON JUNCTION (Grand Union Canal): $49\frac{1}{4}$ miles, 38 locks
BRAUNSTON TURN (Grand Union Canal): $54\frac{1}{4}$ miles, 38 locks
Hillmorton Bottom Lock $61\frac{3}{4}$ miles, 41 locks
Stretton Stop: 70 miles, 41 locks
HAWKESBURY JUNCTION (Coventry Canal): 77 miles, 42 locks

Napton bottom lock, Oxford Canal. *Derek Pratt.*

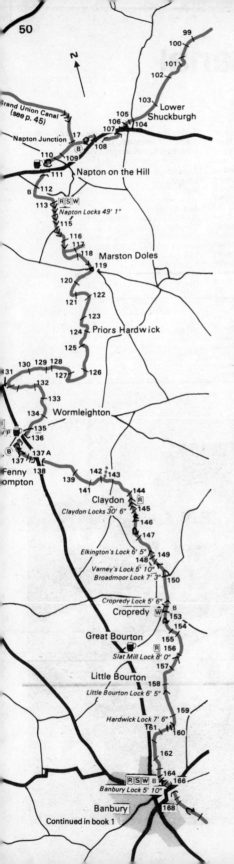

Banbury

23 miles

The canalside housing estates and industrial areas of Banbury soon give way to the more typical Oxford countryside as the canal continues its climb to the summit level at Claydon. Here it follows Brindley's extravagant 'contour' route after passing through the wooded cutting of 'Fenny Compton Tunnel'. At Marston Doles it starts its descent to meet the Grand Union at Napton Junction.

Banbury
Oxon. Pop 28,000. EC Tue. MD Thur/Sat. All services. Banbury is far more attractive than it appears from the canal. Originally a wool town, the castle was pulled down by Cromwell's forces in 1646. The ancient cross of nursery rhyme fame was pulled down in 1602, the present cross is a 19thC replica. The famous spiced Banbury cakes are still produced in the original bake house. See also the Museum and Globe Room.

Little Bourton
Oxon. PO box, tel, garage. Quiet residential village. *Stores* in nearby Great Bourton.

Claydon
Oxon. Pop 202. PO box, tel. An old fashioned brown stone village set in a rolling open landscape. Clattercote Priory, just to the south, still remains. The Claydon Granary Museum contains a fascinating array of relics, which you are welcome to handle, and is well worth the $1\frac{1}{2}$m walk from the canal. There is also a small gift shop. Admission is free.

Cropredy
Oxon. Pop 459. PO, tel, stores, garage. A sleepy village of brick houses close to the canal. Stately sandstone church with fine woodwork. A plaque on the river bridge recalls the Battle of Cropredy, 1644.

Priors Hardwick
Warwicks. Pop 143. PO, tel. Approachable from the canal by footpath. A small village, partly deserted since it was pulled down by the Cistercian monks in the 14thC. Parts of the squat stone church are 13thC.

Wormleighton
Warwicks. Pop 190. PO, tel. A fine manorial village. Its 13thC brown stone church contains a perpendicular screen and Jacobean woodwork.

Fenny Compton
Warwicks. Pop 520. PO, tel, stores, garage. A scattered brown stone village. The church is partly 14thC and partly Victorian; alongside is a fine brick rectory of 1707. Fenny Compton Tunnel is no more, having been converted into a cutting in 1868.

Napton-on-the-Hill
Warwicks. Pop 760. PO, tel, stores, garage. Rising to over 400ft, Napton Hill dominates the immediate landscape, the village climbing steeply up the sides. The shops and pubs are at the bottom. Near the church, alone on the hilltop, is the recently restored windmill.

Marston Doles
Warwicks. Tel, stores. Tiny settlement that owes its existence to the canal. Nearby are the remains of the pumping house which used to pump water to the summit level.

BOATYARDS & BWB

Ⓑ **Cropredy Motor Cycles** by Cropredy Lock. (029 575 386). Ⓦ Pump-out Mon–Sat.

Ⓑ **Fenny Marina** Station Fields, Fenny Compton, Warwicks. (461/2/3). Large marina Ⓡ Ⓢ Ⓦ Ⓟ Ⓓ Moorings, gas, chandlery, pump-out. Lavatories. Slipway, winter storage (hard standing). Manufacturers of steel narrow boats and 20 foot fibreglass boats. *Closed winter weekends.*

Ⓑ **Adkins Cruisers** Holt Farm, Southam, Warwicks. (Southam 2225). Ⓡ Ⓢ Ⓦ Gas, moorings. *Closed winter.*

Ⓑ **A. J. Cruisers** 2 Market Hill, Southam, Warwicks. (Southam 2685). Ⓡ Ⓢ Ⓦ Boat hire, gas, mooring, toilets, provisions.

ⓑ Gordon's Pleasure Cruisers Napton Marina, Stockton, Rugby, Warwicks. (Southam 3644). Steel hire cruisers. ⓡⓢⓦⓓ Pump-out, gas, chandlery, launderette, showers. Slipway, covered wet dock. Moorings. Designers of steel narrow boats. Groceries available. *Open Apr–Oct.*

PUBS & RESTAURANTS

Plough Little Bourton. Food.

Swan Inn Great Bourton (Cropredy 8181).

Red Lion Cropredy. Food.

✗ Brasenose Inn Cropredy (244).

✗ Sunrising Claydon.

✗ George and Dragon Fenny Compton Wharf (322). Canalside. Food *(except Sun)*, B & B, water.

✗ Napton Bridge Inn Napton. (Southam 2466). Canalside. Lunches, dinners. Advisable to book.

Near Fenny Compton, Oxford Canal. *Derek Pratt.*

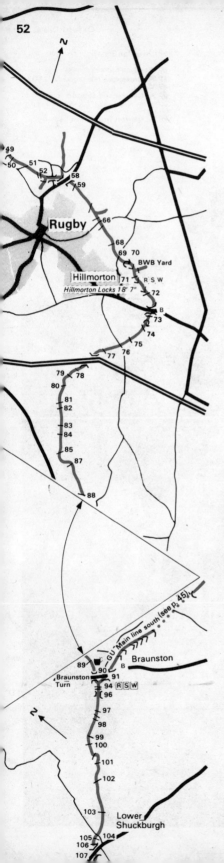

Braunston

15 miles

Leaving Napton, the Oxford Canal shares its route with the Grand Union to Braunston, then bears off to the north towards Rugby, the Grand Union continuing south east. This is open country, with evidence of medieval ridge and furrow field systems on the south bank; there are few villages and the landscape is quiet and empty. Approaching Rugby, radio masts can be seen to the east. The canal descends the three paired narrow locks and passes the attractively sited BWB maintenance yard at Hillmorton before swinging in a wide arc round Rugby.

Lower Shuckburgh
Northants. Pop 74. PO box. A tiny village along the main road. The church, built 1864, is very attractive. A farm, west of bridge 104, sells eggs.

Willoughby
Warwicks. PO, tel, stores, garage, cafe. A mellow red brick village. The small church is dominated by a fine 18thC rectory. Excellent home bakery.

Hillmorton
Warwicks. PO, tel, stores, garage. Its church dates from c.1300, with additions as late as 18thC. There is a medieval cross in the centre of the village.

BOATYARDS & BWB

Ⓑ **BWB Hillmorton Locks** Hillmorton. (Rugby 73149) Ⓡ Ⓢ Ⓦ (Ⓓ emergency only). Mooring, gas, toilets, dry dock, hire cruisers, pump-out. *Facilities Mon–Fri.*

Ⓑ **Rugby Boatbuilders** Hillmorton Wharf, Crick road, Rugby. (4438). Ⓢ Ⓦ Ⓓ Steel narrow boats built, repaired or fitted out. Engines overhauled. Steel hire cruisers available. Gas, dry dock, mooring, chandlers, toilets, gift shop. *Closed winter Suns.*

Ⓑ **Clifton Cruisers** Clifton Wharf, Vicarage Hill, Rugby (3570). Ⓡ Ⓢ Ⓦ Ⓓ Pump-out. Boat hire, gas, repairs, toilets. *Phone first in winter.*

PUBS & RESTAURANTS

🍺 ✕ **The Boatman** Braunston (Rugby 890313). Popular canalside pub at Braunston Turn. Bar snacks, garden with swings. Meals *every day except Sun eve and all day Mon.*

🍺 **Rose Inn** Willoughby.
🍺 **Stag and Pheasant** Hillmorton. Food.
🍺 **Arnold Arms** Barby (1¼ miles S of bridge 76). Food.

Rugby

13 miles

Swinging round Rugby, the canal enters a side cut embankment, then crosses the River Avon on an aqueduct. A short open stretch, then into Newbold Tunnel and a wooded cutting which gives way to fine farming land with small woods, some reaching to the water's edge. Past Brinklow the canal continues along an embankment (formerly an aqueduct, but now filled in) to Stretton before entering another deep cutting. The iron bridges that occur periodically mark the course prior to the 1829 shortening. Approaching Coventry the motorway makes its presence felt, and open land is replaced with pylons and housing. At Hawkesbury Junction, after some sharp bends, the Oxford Canal joins the Coventry.

Rugby
Warwicks. Pop 56,450. EC Wed. MD Mon/Sat. All services. Famous for the Rugby school where Rugby football was first played. The town was important for its agriculture for over 600 years, but today heavy electrical industries determine the character of the area. Visit the Library Exhibition Gallery and Museum, St Matthew st.

Newbold-on-Avon
Warwicks. PO, tel, stores, garage, fish and chips. A pleasant village with an interesting 15thC church. Near the tunnel mouth are two pubs right next door to each other—a fine sight.

Newbold Tunnel
This 250yd long tunnel was built during the shortening of the canal in the 1820's. The old tunnel mouth can be seen from the south by Newbold church.

Harborough Magna
Warwicks. PO, tel, stores. A quiet red brick village. 14thC church with interesting stained glass window.

Brinklow
Warwicks. Pop 1090. PO, tel, stores, garage. A spacious pre-industrial village built along a wide main street. The church is unusual in having a distinctly sloping floor.

Ansty
West Midlands. PO, tel, stores, garage. Tiny village that grew up along the canal. This area has been much altered by the motorway crossing to the south.

Shilton
West Midlands. PO, tel, stores, garage. Main road village left bewildered by the railway and the A46.

BOATYARDS & BWB
Ⓑ **Willow Wren Hire Cruisers** Rugby Wharf, off Consul rd, Leicester rd, Rugby. (4520). Ⓡ Ⓢ Ⓦ Ⓟ Ⓓ Boat hire, gas, boat building and repairs, toilets. *Closed Sun.*

Ⓑ **Rose Narrowboats** Brinklow Marina, Stretton Stop. (Rugby 832449). Ⓡ Ⓦ Ⓟ Ⓓ Moorings, repairs, hire cruisers. Pump-out, gas, chandlery, provisions. Pottery made adjacent to the boatyard.

PUBS & RESTAURANTS
🍺✕ **Three Horseshoes Hotel** Sheep st, Rugby. (4585). Food.
✕❢ **Andalucia Restaurant** 10 Henry st, Rugby. (76404). Good Spanish food. Book.
🍺 **Golden Lion** Harborough Magna. Food.
🍺 **Boat** Newbold Wharf. Canalside. skittles.
🍺 **Barley Mow** Newbold Wharf. Canalside. Food skittles.
🍺 **White Lion** Brinklow. Food.
🍺 **Bull's Head** Brinklow. Food.
🍺 **Raven** Brinklow. Food.
🍺 **Railway Inn** Stretton Stop. Canalside. Food.
🍺 **Crown** Shilton. Food.
🍺 **Crown** Ansty. Food.
🍺 **Elephant and Castle** Canalside. By bridge 4. Food.
🍺 **Greyhound** Hawkesbury Junction. Canalside. Food.

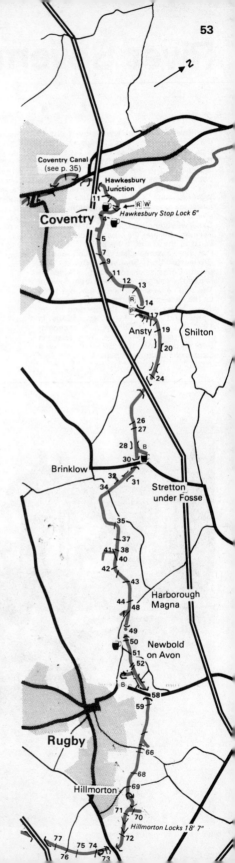

Coventry Canal
(see p. 35)

Hawkesbury Junction

11

Coventry

Ⓡ Ⓦ ← *Hawkesbury Stop Lock 6"*
4

5

7

9

11

12   13

Ⓡ   14
Ⓟ   17

Ansty   19   **Shilton**

)   [20

24

26
27

28)   Ⓑ

30   Ⓑ

Brinklow

32
34   31   **Stretton under Fosse**

35

37

41) 38
40

42

43

44   48   **Harborough Magna**

49

50   **Newbold on Avon**

51

52

Ⓑ

58

59

Rugby

66

68

69

Hillmorton   71   70

72   *Hillmorton Locks 18' 7"*

73

77   75 74

76

River Severn

The River Severn has always been one of the principal navigations in England—at one time boats travelled as far as Welshpool. But with bigger boats the limit of navigation receded, and in the late 18thC the inland port of Bewdley was losing its significance. The opening of the Staffordshire & Worcestershire Canal in 1772 led to measures to improve the navigation, and as a result the Gloucester & Sharpness Ship Canal was completed in 1827. At the time of opening, this was the broadest and deepest canal in the world, a far sighted decision that has ensured the continued use of Gloucester and Sharpness Docks. The Severn Commission, formed in 1874, maintained the navigation of the Upper Severn. The ship canal still remains busy, but trade on the river above Gloucester has dwindled away. However, since the opening of the Upper and Lower Avon Navigations in 1974, the river is part of a fine circular cruising route, with the Worcester & Birmingham and the Stratford-on-Avon Canals completing the ring.

Maximum dimensions
Gloucester to Worcester
Length: 135', Beam: 21'
Headroom: 24'6"
Worcester to Stourport
Length: 90', Beam: 19'
Headroom: 20'
GLOUCESTER Lock to
TEWKESBURY junction with River Avon: 13
DIGLIS junction with Worcester &
Birmingham Canal: 29
STOURPORT junction with Staffs & Worcs
Canal: 42
Total 5 locks

Upton upon Severn. *Derek Pratt.*

Tewkesbury

21 miles

Leaving Wainlode Hill behind, the river winds towards Tewkesbury where it is joined by the Warwickshire Avon (see p. 19). The river is tidal to here on spring tides. The town of Tewkesbury is separated from the river by a flat expanse of meadow, and navigators wishing to visit should proceed east up the Avon (entrance ABOVE Tewkesbury Lock). Above here the river resumes its usual character, isolated by high banks and trees until Upton upon Severn is reached with its interesting waterfront and many boats. Just west of Severn Stoke, tall red cliffs rise straight from the water, then caravans and bungalows appear interspersed along the banks as the river approaches Worcester.

Deerhurst
Glos. Tel. stores. The beautiful church of St. Mary, parts of which date from 804, has one of the best preserved Saxon fonts in England. Odda's Chapel, 200yds SW of the church, is Anglo Saxon, dating from 1056. It was used as part of a farmhouse until rediscovered in 1885. Difficult access from the river over rocky banks.

Haw Bridge
Two pubs and a new bridge to replace the old one knocked down by a barge in 1958.

Coombe Hill Canal
Built in 1796 to carry coal to Cheltenham, and abandoned in 1876, it was recently purchased by the Severn & Canal Carrying Company at auction for £35,000. The 3 mile canal and its buildings are being restored to their original state.

Tewkesbury
Glos. Pop 8500. EC Thur. MD Wed, Sat. All services. Historic town at the junction of the Rivers Avon and Severn. Fine ancient buildings and many tiny alleys leading off the main street; Baptist Chapel Court leads to one of the oldest Baptist Chapels in England (1655). There are many historic pubs and of course **Tewkesbury Abbey,** completed 1120 and thought to be one of the finest Norman churches in the country. Cathedral-like in its proportions, it has a beautifully decorated central tower, 46ft square and over 130ft high. See also the Abbey Cottages dating from 1450, quite unique and beautifully restored; the museum; Barton Fair *in October* and the Steam Fair and Organ Festival *in July.*

Upton upon Severn
Worcs. Pop 2000. EC Thur. PO, tel, stores, garage. A delightful town, and doubly welcome for being right on the river bank. Interesting timbered and Georgian buildings and 13thC church tower. A good point from which to visit Malvern and the Hills, some six miles to the west. Temporary mooring at the Public Quay or Upton Marina (for a small charge).

Ripple
Worcs. PO, tel, stores. Pretty village with a fine church dating from late 12thC.

Severn Stoke
Worcs. PO, tel, stores. Half timbered pub and church with a curious 14thC side tower.

Hanley Castle
Worcs. Pop 1200. PO, tel, stores. No 13thC castle but a pretty village around a green. Church half 14thC stone, half 17thC brick. Access by lane from the river but mooring is tricky.

Kempsey
Worcs. Pop 1700. PO, tel, stores. A grand church built for the Bishop of Worcester. Some cottages among acres of new housing.

BOATYARDS & BWB
Ⓡ **Tewkesbury Marine Services**
St Mary's lane, Tewkesbury (292187). On the Mill Avon. Ⓡ Ⓢ Ⓦ Ⓓ Pump-out *(not Sat).* Boat hire, gas, boat building, boat and engine repairs, mooring, toilets, winter storage.

Continued in book 1

Ⓑ **Upton Marina** Upton upon Severn,
Worcs (Upton 3111) Ⓡ Ⓢ Ⓦ Ⓟ Ⓓ
Pump-out. Slipway, gas, dry dock, repairs,
mooring, chandlery, toilets. Upton
Narrowboats and Corsair Cruisers are
based here.
BWB Diglis Maintenance Yard Diglis
Lock (Worcester 356264)
Ⓑ **Seaborn Yacht Company** Court
Meadow, Kempsey, Worcs (Worcester
820295). Ⓡ Ⓢ Ⓦ Pump-out (*not Sat*).
Boat hire, slipway, gas, boat-building and
repairs, mooring, toilets, showers, winter
storage. *Closed winter Suns.*

BOAT TRIPS

The 'Avon Belle', a former South Coast
boat, runs day trips up and down the Rivers
Avon and Severn, starting on the Mill Avon
at Tewkesbury. Public service, and private
charter trips (maximum 47 passengers).
Enquiries to Mrs Rebane, 185 Queens rd,
Tewkesbury, Glos. (294088). Small self-
drive boats may also be hired from here,
by the hour or by the day. Issues BWB
River Registration and short term licences.
Public slipway nearby. Also weekly cruiser
hire.

PUBS

🍺 **New Bridge** Haw Bridge.
🍺 **Haw Bridge Inn** Guess.
🍺✕ **Coal House** on east bank of river
near Apperley. Food.
🍺✕ **Yew Tree Inn** on west bank of river,
opposite Deerhurst. Large pub at the end of
a lane. Food.
Plenty of excellent pubs and hotels in
Tewkesbury, though none on the River Avon
itself.
🍺 **Lower Lode** on the Severn, ¾ of a mile
below Tewkesbury Lock. Food. Slipway by
the pub, floating moorings. Issues BWB
River Registration and short term licences.
🍺 **Railway Inn** Ripple.
🍺✕ **Star Hotel** Upton. Old free house
near the river. Lunches and dinners daily.
Residential. (Upton 2300).

🍺 **Ye Olde Anchor Inn** Upton, near the
church. This pub is dated 1601.
🍺 **Three Kings** Hanley Castle. Food,
B&B. (Upton upon Severn 2686).
🍺 **Rose & Crown** Severn Stoke.

Severn

Worcester

14 miles

Just above Diglis Locks are the disused
wharves and the two locks that lead into
Diglis Basin and the Worcester &
Birmingham Canal (see p74). The riverside
in Worcester is attractive, overlooked by
the cathedral. From here to Stourport the
surroundings are pleasant, the river running
through a valley with wooded hills, well
tended locks and roads at a distance. There
is an unexpected outcrop of red sandstone
before Stourport with its abandoned
wharves. The Staffordshire &
Worcestershire Canal joins here from the
east. Navigation is possible to within one
mile of Bewdley, given suitable conditions.

Worcester
Pop 71,000. EC Thur. MD Sat. All services.
Known worldwide for its brown sauce and
porcelain. Traffic plagues the place, but the
area around Friar street and of course the
Cathedral are of interest.
The Cathedral Dates from 1074, with work
of five subsequent centuries, a wealth of
stained glass and many fine monuments.
The Purbeck marble effigy of King John
(1216) is the oldest royal effigy in England.
The Commandery Kings Head Lock. Dates
from 15thC. Superb galleried Hall. *Open
daily.*
**Dyson Perrins Museum of Worcester
Porcelain** Severn st (23221). The most

Tardebigge top lock, Worcester & Birmingham Canal. *Derek Pratt.*

Worcester (cont)

comprehensive collection in the world.
Open Mon-Fri, Sats May-Sep.
See also Tudor House Folk Museum *(closed Thur & Sun)*; the Guildhall 1721-3 with its elaborate façade; City Museum and Art Gallery *(closed Sun)*; Greyfriars, one of the finest half-timbered houses in the country.

Holt

Worcs. PO, tel, stores. Assorted settlements scattered around the river. Telford Bridge 1828. The 'castle' tower is 14thC; the church is a fine late Norman building.

Grimley

Worcs. PO, tel, stores. A small farming village hidden from the river.

The Droitwich Canal

An attractive rural waterway being restored by the local Droitwich council and the Droitwich Canal Trust.

The Burf

An isolated settlement for the retired.

Stourport

Worcs. Pop 15,000. EC Wed. All services. This town owes its existence to the Stafford-shire & Worcestershire Canal which joins the Severn here. The canal company built the basins, locks, warehouses, workers cottages (esp. Mart lane), the clock tower and even the Tontine Hotel (still licensed). In contrast to the 'canal' area, the rest of the town seems dull.

Bewdley

Worcs. A superb 18thC riverside town well worth the trip from Stourport. Time your journey to coincide with licensing hours, and have a ride on the Severn Valley Steam Railway nearby.

BOATYARDS & BWB

ⓑ **Hoskins Marina** Dunley rd, Stourport on Severn. (2786). **R** **S** **W** Pump-out. Slipway, dry dock, boat building & repair, mooring, toilets, winter storage, dingy day hire.

BOAT TRIPS

Severn Steamboat Co. Trips from Stourport to Worcester and back on *Weds July & Aug.* Also trips on the river *mid summer* according to demand and boat charter. Details Stourport 71177.

PUBS

There are plenty in Worcester.

🍺 **Camp House Inn** Grimley. An isolated riverside pub below Bevere Lock. Food. Good moorings. (Worcester (640288). The drinking water here is pumped up electrically from a well.
🍺 **Holt Fleet Hotel** Holt Fleet.
🍺 **Lenchford** Holt. Riverside.
🍺 **Hempstall Cider House** The Burf. Good moorings. Food (and beers).
🍺 **Tontine Hotel** Stourport Basin.
🍺 **Black Boy** Bewdley. Unspoilt.
🍺 **Rising Sun** Bewdley. Small.

TOURIST INFORMATION CENTRE

Worcester The Guildhall, Worcester. (23471).

Staffs & Worcs
(see p. 61)

Bewdley

Limit of navigation

Stourport

Stourport Basins
B
S W

Lincomb Lock
7'4"

The Burf

Holt Lock 5'3"

Holt

Grimley

Bevere Lock
5'1"

Droitwich Canal

Worcester & Birmingham Canal (see p. 74)

Worcester

Diglis Basin
B
BWB Diglis Yard
Diglis Locks
S
7'11"

River Soar

The Soar is a tributary of the Trent. It was made navigable to Loughborough in 1778, bringing great prosperity to the town. The navigation was then extended to Leicester and the first boats arrived there on 21 February 1794. The Loughborough Navigation was one of the most prosperous canals in England, by virtue of its relationship to the Nottinghamshire/Derbyshire coalfield and the Erewash Canal. Both navigations were purchased by the Grand Union in 1931.

Maximum dimensions
Leicester West Bridge to River Trent
Length: 72', Beam: 14' 4", Headroom: 7' 6"
Mileage
LEICESTER West Bridge to
Barrow upon Soar: 12
RIVER TRENT: 25
Total 18 locks

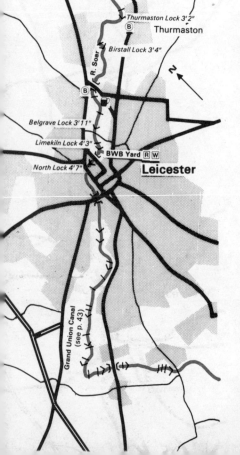

2 miles

It is just south of Leicester that the Leicester Branch of the Grand Union Canal main line is intercepted by the River Soar. It is worth remembering that the River Soar floods frequently in heavy rain, so boatmen travelling out of season should enquire about the navigational conditions in advance.
For almost all of its journey through the city of Leicester, the navigation pursues a course quite separate from the river, the navigation having been rebuilt towards the end of the 19thC as part of Leicester's flood prevention scheme. For half a mile south of West Bridge, the navigation is like a formal avenue, tree-lined and crossed by several ornamental iron bridges but where it curves under the old Great Central railway the navigation begins to follow a less public course through the nether regions of Leicester. A combination of locks, derelict canal basins, tall factory buildings and a substantial stretch of parkland adds up to a stretch of urban canal that offers a greater variety of interest than exists in most other cities. At Belgrave Lock the canal joins the Soar, which proceeds to meander carelessly through the city's outskirts. Fortunately the broad margin of water meadows succeeds in keeping these at arm's length for most of the way.

Leicester
For details see page 43.

BOATYARDS & BWB

ⓑ **Charnwood Marine** (Mill Lane Boatyard), Thurmaston, Leics. (693069). Ⓡ Ⓢ Ⓦ Ⓓ Pump-out. Boat hire, slipway, gas, boat building & repair, mooring, chandlery, toilets, showers, winter storage.
ⓑ **Leicester Marina** Old Bridge, Thurcaston rd (Leicester 62194). Ⓢ Ⓦ Ⓓ Pump-out. Gas, mooring, slipway, chandlery, boat building & repairs, toilets, winter storage. Trip boat for charter.
ⓑ **BWB Leicester Yard** Belgrave Gate (Leicester 59512) Ⓡ Ⓦ

PUBS

🍺 **Joiners Arms** Sanrey Gate, Leicester. SE of North Bridge.
🍺 **Richmond Arms** King Richards rd, Leicester. W of West Bridge.

Loughborough

23 miles

At Thurmaston Lock there is a boatyard, with shops and a pub nearby. The canal then heads north through gravel workings, followed by more natural surroundings. There is a fine old mill by Cossington Lock, and below here the river is flanked by low green hills and water meadows to Mountsorrel, where there is a lock, a pub and two boatyards. The river then meanders across the valley to the pretty village of Barrow upon Soar. A short canal section bypasses a wide sweep in the river, and contains a very deep lock. There is then a short wooded stretch as the navigation passes through Pillings Flood Lock the gates are usually open. This pleasant landscape is soon replaced by Loughborough and the back wall of an engineering works. The canal skirts the town to a 'T' junction where the Leicester Navigation ends and the Loughborough Navigation starts turn right. The navigation passes through open country to Normanton on Soar, where access from the river is poor, then on to Zouch, where it is better and there are more facilities. At Devil's Elbow boats heading downstream should keep to the *right* to stay in the main channel at the start of another pleasant meandering stretch. Approaching Kegworth there is a maze of backwaters: keep to the *right* for Kegworth Deep Lock. After a sharp swing to the north, navigators should again keep *right* for Kegworth Shallow Lock. From here to the Trent the navigation becomes more isolated, but two notable landmarks are the spire of Ratcliffe on Soar church and the cooling towers of Ratcliffe Power Station, both to the east. The last lock on the navigation, Redhill, has beautifully kept lawns and a well painted bridge. Below here the river joins the Trent, make sure you turn LEFT, as Thrumpton Weir is to the right.

Thurmaston
Leics. PO, tel. stores, garage. An unexciting suburb of Leicester. In 1955, evidence of Roman habitation was discovered here.

Cossington
Leics. PO, tel. A mile east of the lock and mill. A pretty, well kept village. The church has excellent Victorian stained glass.

Rothley
Leics. Pop 3800. PO, tel, stores garage. One mile west of Cossington Lock. A 13thC chapel with a figure of a Knight Templar remains by the Elizabethan House, once the home of the Babington family, birthplace of Lord Macaulay and now an hotel. The Norman church in the village is mainly granite.

Mountsorrel
Leics. Pop 4000. PO, tel, stores, garage. Close by the lock. Bisected by the A6, but the dignity of the old buildings survives. There is a covered market cross. The church and the vicarage face each other across the road. In the hills behind the village, the pinkish Mountsorrel granite is quarried.

Wreake Navigation & the Oakham Canal
Opened in 1795 to connect the Soar below Syston to Melton Mowbray, and Oakham in Rutland. The Oakham closed in 1846 and the Wreake in 1877.

Barrow upon Soar
Leics. Pop 4000. PO, tel, stores, garage. Very pretty near the old stone bridge and the lock. Popular in summer.

Loughborough
Leics. Pop 40,000. EC Wed. MD Thur/Sat. All services. A busy industrial town, known for the bells cast here by John Taylor & Co for over a century. One of their largest is Great Paul in St Paul's Cathedral, London. The town war memorial is a Carillon Tower.

Normanton on Soar
Notts. PO, tel. A quiet, preserved and discreetly pretty village. The post office is

timbered and thatched (unusual around here), and the cruciform church has a central tower and a spire, again unusual for so small a church. Inside are some excellent stone carvings.

Whatton House
Visible from near Devil's Elbow. Built 1802 and restored in 1876 after a fire. Its fine 25 acre garden is *open Sun afternoons in the summer.*

Kegworth
Leics. PO, tel, stores, bank. Attractively sited on a hill, topped by the church spire, it remains better viewed at a distance.

Kingston on Soar
Notts. PO, tel, stores. A small estate village with a pretty church.

Ratcliffe on Soar
Notts. PO, tel, stores. A tiny village with a spired church dating from 13thC, the interior of which is pleasantly uncluttered, with whitewashed walls accentuating the bold ancient arches.

BOATYARDS & BWB

Ⓑ **Soar Valley Boatyard** Sileby rd, Mountsorrel, Leics. (Leicester 302642). Chandlery (also clothing), slipway, moorings. Boat sales & repairs. *Open daily.*

Ⓑ **Mountsorrel Marine Centre (Ladyline)** 14-18 Loughborough rd, Mountsorrel, Leics. (Leicester 302144). Gas, chandlery, toilets, showers.

Ⓑ **L. R. Harris & Son** Old Junction Boatyard, Meadow lane, Syston, near Leicester. (Leicester 692135). Ⓡ Ⓦ Ⓟ Ⓓ Gas, chandlery, slipway, winter storage, Boat sales & repairs, inboard and outboard engines sales & repairs. Welding specialists. *Open daily.*

Ⓑ **BWB Loughborough Yard** (Loughborough 22729) Ⓡ Ⓦ

Ⓑ **Kegworth Marine** Kingston lane, Kegworth, Leics. (Kegworth 2300). Moorings, gas, repairs, winter storage.

Ⓑ **Sileby River Services** Mountsorrel lane, Sileby (3404) Ⓡ Ⓢ Ⓦ Ⓓ Pumpout. Hire fleet, slipway, moorings, gas, chandlery, groceries, café, toilets. Boat building & repairs, winter storage.

PUBS & RESTAURANTS

🍺 **Hope & Anchor** Syston. Canalside, good moorings.

🍺 **Royal Oak** Cossington.

✖🍷 **Cossington Mill** by Cossington Lock (Sileby 2205). This oak-beamed converted mill has stood beside the River Soar for 700 years. A short menu includes steak, chicken Simla, pork sanglier. *Closed Sat L and Sun.* Book.

🍺✖ **Red Lion** Rothley, at crossroads up the hill west of Cossington Lock. Restaurant meals *daily except Sun dinner.* (Rothley 2655).

🍺✖ **Waterside Inn** Mountsorrel Lock (Rothley 2758). Bar snacks, restaurant *meals daily, except Sat lunch and Sun dinner* (last sitting 21.30).

🍺 **Navigation** Barrow upon Soar. Canalside, garden.

🍺 **Soar Bridge Inn** Barrow upon Soar. Near the river bridge. Food. Petrol nearby.

🍺 **Albion** Loughborough. Canalside, on towpath just north of the junction.

🍺 **Boat** Loughborough. Canalside, at bridge east of junction.

🍺 **Duke of York** Loughborough. Canalside at the bridge near the station. Grocer and fish & chips nearby.

🍺✖ **Plough** Normanton. (Hathern 228). Large old riverside pub with a garden and restaurant.

🍺 **Rose and Crown** Zouch. Canalside.

🍺 **Anchor** Sutton Bonington.

🍺✖ **White House** riverside, south of Kegworth. Bar meals most days.

🍺 **Anchor** Kegworth, near Shallow Lock. Food.

Good moorings at Sandiacre.

Staffordshire & Worcestershire

Construction was begun immediately after that of the Trent & Mersey to effect the joining of the Rivers Trent, Mersey and Severn. Engineered by James Brindley, it opened in 1772, 46 miles in length from Great Haywood on the T & M to the River Severn at Stourport (a town that owed its birth and rapid growth to the canal). Following its initial success, the S & W soon found itself facing strong competition from the Worcester & Birmingham Canal which offered a more direct link between Birmingham and the Severn, and also from the Birmingham & Liverpool Junction, which connected more directly with Merseyside. However, by levying absurdly high tolls on the vital and much used ½ mile between Autherley and Aldersley Junctions the S & W protected its position, although the threat of a 'by-pass' canal finally forced the profiteering S & W to reduce its charges to a more acceptable level. Like other narrow canals, its trade declined with the coming of the railways, but its future is assured as a cruising waterway.

Maximum dimensions
Autherley to Great Haywood
Length: 72'
Beam: 7'
Headroom: 7'
Mileage
STOURPORT to:
Kidderminster lock: 4½
Wolverley lock: 6
STOURTON JUNCTION: 12¼
Swindon: 16¾
Bratch locks: 19
ALDERSLEY JUNCTION: 25
AUTHERLEY JUNCTION: 25½
GREAT HAYWOOD JUNCTION: 46

3½ miles

The canal starts in the east corner of the upper basins of Stourport (see detailed map on the next page) and immediately negotiates the very deep York Street Lock. It then creeps through Stourport flanked by mellow buildings and a rural towpath, before entering the country. The navigation then proceeds along a pretty little valley before passing a sewage works. The sweet smells here are incentive enough for the navigator to press on towards Kidderminster which is approached alongside a dramatic red cliff rising sheer from the water's edge. Falling Sands and Caldwell Locks are delightfully situated at the foot of this geological feature, and both have Stratford on Avon Canal type split bridges. The canal's course through Kidderminster is a private one until a short tunnel opens out into pleasant townscape. This in turn is followed by modern industrial works, which eventually give way to the quiet watermeadows of the River Stour. Beyond Wolverley Lock the course of the canal is very narrow, hemmed in by steep cliffs of friable red sandstone covered in a tangle of foliage. The navigation winds tortuously through these surroundings which culminate in Austcliff Rock, leaning unnervingly out over the water. Now the rocks are replaced by thick woods.

Stourport
Worcs. Pop 15,000. EC Wed. All services.
This town owes its existence to the Staffordshire & Worcestershire Canal which joins the Severn here. The canal company built the basins, locks, warehouses, workers' cottages (esp. Mart lane), the clock tower and even the Tontine Hotel (still licensed). In contrast to the 'canal' area, the rest of the town seems dull.

Kidderminster
Worcs. Pop 47,000. EC Wed. MD Thur. Cat. All services. There are few buildings of interest in this town, which exists above all for carpet making. Perhaps the older industrial part, visible from the canal, is the best. Access is easiest from Kidderminster Lock, where the public baths are conveniently sited. The Museum and Art Gallery in Market st have items of local interest, and some Brangwyn etchings

Wolverley
Worcs. PO, tel, stores. A pretty village clustered to the north of a steep sandstone rock, on top of which stands the dark red Italianate style church, built 1772. The grammar school, endowed in 1629, is dignified, and gardens make the most of the brook that flows through. There are two nice pubs in this unusual village which is easily accessible from Wolverley Lock.

Cookley
Worcs. PO, tel, stores, garage, fish & chips. The canal passes underneath this village in a tunnel. There are some attractive old cottages down by the Stour, and some caves are clearly visible in the cliff face, but the village has little else to offer.

Caunsall
Worcs. A small farming settlement.

BOATYARDS & BWB

Ⓑ BWB Stourport Yard Stourport Basin (2838) Ⓡ Ⓢ Ⓦ close by.

Ⓑ Dartline Parkes passage, off York st, Stourport on Severn. (2970) Ⓡ Ⓢ Ⓦ Ⓓ Pump-out *(Mon–Fri)*. Boat hire, mooring, toilets, winter storage.

Ⓑ Heads Boatshop Stourport Basin (2044) Ⓡ Ⓢ Ⓦ Slipway, gas, dry dock, mooring, chandlery, toilets, provisions.

Ⓑ Severn Valley Cruisers York st Boatyard, Stourport (71165). Ⓡ Ⓦ Ⓓ Pump-out *(not Sat)*. Boat hire, slipway, gas, boat building & repair, mooring, chandlery, toilets, winter storage.

Ⓑ Cleaver Marine Engine Lane, Stourport (77222). Ⓡ Ⓦ Ⓓ Pump-out. Boat hire, boat building & repair, toilet. *Closed winter weekends.*

PUBS

🍺 **Tontine Hotel** Stourport Basin.

🍺 **Bell Hotel** Stourport, opposite York Street Lock.

🍺 **White Lion** near the Bell.

🍺 **Black Star** Stourport, Canalside, by bridge 5.

🍺 **Bird in Hand** Stourport, Canalside, south of the railway bridge.

🍺 **Chester Tavern** Chester rd, Kidderminster.

🍺 **Lock** Canalside, at Wolverley Lock Terrace fronting the canal. Food usually available.

🍺 **Queens Head** Wolverley, near the old school. Terrace.

🍺 **Bulls Head** Cookley. Up the hill from the tunnel, near the shops.

🍺 **Rock** Caunsall, ¼ mile W of bridge 26.

🍺 **Queens Head** Caunsall, near the Rock.

STOURPORT BASINS.

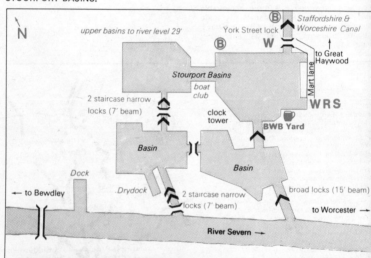

Wolverley, Staffordshire & Worcestershire. *Derek Pratt.*

Bratch Locks

20¼ miles

The canal passes from Worcestershire into
Staffordshire after bridge 26, but the
surroundings remain the same - secluded
woodlands with a rocky hillside on the east
bank punctuated with pretty cottages and
locks. Beyond Dunsley Tunnel (a rough-
hewn bore), and Stewponey Lock with its
restored octagonal toll office, is Stourton
Junction, where the Stourbridge Canal
leaves to connect with the BCN (see p32
of this book). The navigation then
winds extravagantly alongside Smeestow
Brook. A narrow entrance on the right
beyond bridge 36 leads to Ashwood Basin
and a boatyard. North of Rocky Lock the
countryside becomes flatter and more
regular, but the canal itself remains delightful. North of Botterham Locks the surroundings are less rural. The unique and attractive
Bratch Locks raise the canal 30ft, and the
view along the valley from here is excellent.
The canal now skirts the W of Wolverhampton
to Compton Lock and the summit level,
having climbed some 294ft from Stourport.
At Aldersley Junction the main line of the
Birmingham Canal climbs away up the
21 Wolverhampton Locks (see p26
of this book) to Birmingham. Half a mile
further along the Shropshire Union branches
off NW (book 3) at Autherley Junction.
Wolverhampton aerodrome is passed, after
which the navigation enters a very narrow
cutting through rock. It then leaves the
suburbs of Wolverhampton behind and
winds through pleasant open country.

Kinver
Staffs. PO, tel, stores, garage. A very pretty
village, nestling among tall wooded hills.
The church is near Kinver Edge, a
tremendous ridge covered in gorse and
heather, lying to the W.
Stourton Castle
W of Stewponey Lock. A curious mixture
of building styles and materials. Birthplace
of Cardinal Pole in 1500. Private.
Swindon
Staffs. PO, tel, stores, fish & chips. An old
farming village, with a 19thC ironworks near
the canal.
Bratch Locks
Attractively sited, with an octagonal toll
office; these locks have an unusual layout.
The pounds between the top gate of one
lock and the bottom of the next seem
impossibly short, but side ponds, hidden
behind the hedge, connect with the pounds,
and are the secret of their operation. Just
treat them as ordinary locks, *making sure
gates and paddles are closed as you go.* They
are *not* staircase locks.
Wightwick
Staffs. (Pronounced 'Wittick'). Pleasant by
the canal bridge and the pub. Wightwick
Manor, 300yds NW of bridge 56, was built
between 1887 and 1893, and has some fine
interior furnishing. *Open afternoons Thur,
Sat & B Hol weekends, also Wed May-Sept.*
Compton
Staffs. PO, tel, stores, launderette.
A busy but uninteresting village.
Tettenhall
West Midlands. PO, tel, stores, garage. A
residential suburb of Wolverhampton. The
battlemented tower of the Norman church
300yds N of bridge 61 is worth a visit.
Coven
Staffs. PO, tel, stores, garage, launderette.
Good for shopping.

BOATYARDS & BWB
Ⓑ **Kinver Lock Marina** The Paddock,
Kinver, Staffs. (2363) Ⓡ Ⓢ Ⓦ Ⓟ Ⓓ
Pump-out. Boat hire, slipway, gas, boat
building & repair, mooring, chandlery,
toilets, provisions, winter storage, licensed
club & restaurant. *Closed winter weekends.*
Ⓑ **Mermaid Hire Cruisers** Wightwick
Wharf, Castlecroft, Wolverhampton
(763818). By bridge 56. Hire cruisers,
engine and boat repairs. Groceries and fuel
nearby. Mooring.
Ⓑ **Water Travel** Autherley Junction,
Oxley Moore rd, Wolverhampton, West

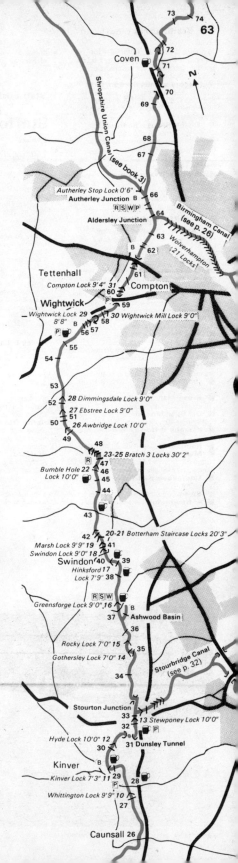

63

Autherley Stop Lock 0'6"
Autherley Junction Ⓡ Ⓢ Ⓦ Ⓟ
Aldersley Junction

Birmingham Canal
(see p. 26)

Wolverhampton
21 Locks

Tettenhall

Compton Lock 9'4" 31
Compton

Wightwick
Wightwick Lock 29
8'8"   30 Wightwick Mill Lock 9'0"

28 Dimmingsdale Lock 9'0"
27 Ebstree Lock 9'0"
26 Awbridge Lock 10'0"

Ⓡ   23-25 Bratch 3 Locks 30'2"
Bumble Hole 22
Lock 10'0"

20-21 Botterham Staircase Locks 20'3"

Marsh Lock 9'9" 19
Swindon Lock 9'0" 18
Swindon
Hinksford 17
Lock 7'9" 38

Ⓡ Ⓢ Ⓦ
Greensforge Lock 9'0" 16
Ashwood Basin

Rocky Lock 7'0" 15
Gothersley Lock 7'0" 14

Stourbridge Canal
(see p. 32)

Stourton Junction
13 Stewponey Lock 10'0"

Hyde Lock 10'0" 12
31 Dunsley Tunnel

Kinver
Kinver Lock 7'3" 11

Whittington Lock 9'9" 10

Caunsall 26

Shropshire Union Canal (see book 3)

Coven

Midlands (782371). R S W P D
Pump-out. Boat hire, slipway, gas, boat
building & repair, mooring, chandlery,
toilets, provisions, cranage.
Ⓑ **Gregory's Canal Cruisers** Oxley Moor
Road Bridge, Autherly Junction, Wolverhampton (783070). R W :Hire fleet, steel
boats built and fitted. Gas, chandlery, toilets,
provisions.
Ⓑ **Double Pennant Boatyard** Hordern
rd, Wolverhampton. (753453). R W D
Boat hire, slipway, gas, engine repairs,
mooring, chandlery, toilets.

BOAT TRIPS
Narrowboat 'Water Tripper' is available
for parties of up to 42. All enquiries to
Party Line, Newbridge Wharf,
Tettenhall rd, Wolverhampton, West Mids.
(Wolverhampton 757494).

PUBS & RESTAURANTS
✕❢ **Anchor** 200yds W of bridge 28.
15thC residential inn–dinners and Sun
lunches, *daily throughout the year*. No public
bar. (Kinver 2085 and 3291).
🍺✕ **Whittington** 300yds E of bridge 28,
along a footpath. Dating from 1300, this
pub was the home of Dick Whittington's
grandfather, and much later of Lady Jane
Grey, whose ghost is sometimes encountered
in the inn. There are also priest holes and
a tunnel to the nearby Whittington Hall.
Restaurant meals served here *daily except
Sun*. Reservations to Kinver 2110.
🍺 **Vine** by Kinver Lock.
🍺 **Ye Old White Hart** Kinver.
🍺✕ **Stewponey & Foley Arms** 50yds
E of Stewponey Lock. Steak house.
🍺 **Navigation** Greensforge. Canalside, at
the lock. Snacks and local draught beer.
🍺 **Old Bush** Hinksford, 100yds NE of
bridge 38. Garden.
🍺 **Green Man** Swindon Ironworks,
100yds W of bridge 40.
🍺 **Old Bush Inn** Swindon village, 150yds
E of bridge 40.
🍺 **Waggon & Horses** Near the canal at
bridge 43, on B4176.
🍺 **Round Oak** Canalside, at bridge 45.
🍺 **Mermaid** Wightwick, 50yds NW of
bridge 56. *Lunches Mon-Sat, 12.00-14.00.*
Sandwiches usually obtainable.
🍺 **Oddfellows Hall** Compton, 50yds W of
bridge 59.
🍺 **Swan** Compton, near the Oddfellows.
🍺✕ **Newbridge** Tettenhall, 50yds E of

bridge 61. Food. The inn sign is a picture
of Thomas Telford.

Staffordshire & Worcestershire

Stafford

17 miles

Hatherton Junction marks the entrance to
the Hatherton Branch, which used to connect with the BCN; it is now unnavigable but
acts as a feeder. Travelling N, the small
canal settlement of Gailey Wharf, with its
large round tollkeeper's watch-tower, is
reached. The canal then descends 5 locks
to Penkridge, the motorway never far away
and an unwelcome intruder in what would
otherwise be a quiet and pleasant river
valley. At Acton Trussell the motorway at
last roars away, leaving Deptmore Lock in
blissful isolation and peace. After Weeping
Cross, the canal follows the pretty Sow
valley. The view from Tixall Lock is impressive, and the stretch beyond here, to
Great Haywood Junction, is charming and
unusual, passing through the lovely Tixall
Wide and overlooked by Tixall Gatehouse.
The Trent is then crossed on an aqueduct,
and the Trent & Mersey Canal is joined at
the junction (see p73).

Gailey & Calf Heath Reservoirs
Half mile E of Gailey Wharf. Canal feeder
reservoirs and nature reserves. There is a
heronry in Gailey lower reservoir.
Penkridge
*Staffs. Pop 3400. EC Wed. MD Mon. PO,
tel, stores, garage.* An old village with
a tall and sombre church, mostly 12thC,
restored in the 1880's. Inside is a fine
Dutch wrought-iron screen.
Acton Trussell
Staffs. PO, tel, stores. Best seen from
the canal, which is overlooked by the 15thC
church.
Stafford
*Staffs. Pop 54,000. EC Wed. MD Tue,
Fri, Sat. All services.* A town with a wealth
of old buildings in the centre. Fine market
square; Italianate City Hall complex c1880;
a robust gaol and the well sited St. Mary's
Church are all pleasing. There are pretty back

Great Haywood Junction Bridge. *Derek Pratt*

Stafford (cont)

alleys, esp. Church lane. The Museum &
Art Gallery, The Green, has an exhibition of
local history. The town was once connected
to the S & W by a branch that was the
canalised course of the River Sow - this
makes a pleasant walk to the town from
near bridge 100.

Milford
Staffs. PO, tel, stores, garage. Access from
bridge 106. An estate village with a large
green. Milford Hall is hidden by trees.

Tixall
Staffs. PO, tel, stores. A quiet and unspoilt
hamlet facing the wooded slopes of
Cannock Chase. Just to the east are the
stables and the Gatehouse (visible from
Tixall Wide) of the long-vanished Tixall
Hall. This massive square Elizabethan build-
ing is fully 4 storeys high, standing alone in a
field; one can only wonder at the size of the
former hall with a gatehouse as huge as this.
It has recently been restored and is available
for holiday letting. Details from the
Landmark Trust, Shottesbrooke,
Maidenhead, Berks.

BOATYARDS & BWB

Ⓑ **Gailey Marine** The Wharf, Watling st,
Staffs. (Standeford 790612) Ⓡ Ⓢ Ⓦ Ⓓ
Pump-out. Boat hire, gas, boat building &
repair, mooring, toilets. *Closed winter Suns.*
Ⓑ **Teddesley Boating Centre** Park Gate
Lock, Teddesley rd, Penkridge, Staffs.
(4692) Ⓡ Ⓦ Ⓓ Pump-out. Boat hire, gas,
boat & engine repairs, mooring, chandlery,
toilets, winter storage, cranage. *Closed Sun
Dec & Jan.*
Ⓑ **Bijou Line** Penkridge Wharf, Cannock
rd, Penkridge, Staffs (2732). At Penkridge
Lock. Ⓦ Pump-out. Boat hire, gas, boat
building. *Closed in winter.*
Ⓑ **Anglo Welsh Narrowboats** The Canal
Wharf, Mill lane, Great Haywood, Staffs.
(Little Haywood 711). At Great Haywood
Junction Ⓡ Ⓢ Ⓦ Ⓓ Pump-out
(*Mon–Fri*). Boat hire, boat & engine repairs,
mooring, toilets.

PUBS

Ⓟ **Cross Keys** Canalside, at Filance bridge
84. An attractive canal pub Ⓦ
Ⓟ **Boat** Canalside, by Penkridge Lock.
Ⓟ **Horse & Jockey** Penkridge.
Ⓟ✕ **Littleton Arms** Penkridge. (2287).
Food; B&B.
Ⓟ✕ **Bear Inn** Greengate, Stafford
(51070).
Ⓟ **Chains** Martin st, Stafford.
Ⓟ **Nag's Head** Mill st, Stafford.
Ⓟ✕ **Vine Hotel** Salter st, Stafford
(51071). Restaurant: lunches and dinners
(*except Sat evening & Sun*). B&B.
Ⓟ✕ **Trumpet** Canalside, at Radford
bridge. Grills.
Ⓟ **Barley Mow** Milford. Steak bar.

Stratford-on-Avon

Following an Act of Parliament passed in 1793, work began on the canal and progress was rapid. However money ran out after 3 years, and it took 4 years and another Act of Parliament to get things going again. By 1803 the canal was open from King's Norton junction to the junction with the Warwick & Birmingham Canal (now part of the Grand Union Main Line). Cutting started again in 1812, and the route was revised in 1815 to include the present junction with the River Avon at Stratford. The canal was prosperous for a while, but by 1835 it was suffering from railway competition, and despite opposition, its sale to the Great Western Railway was completed in 1856. There was a gradual decline in traffic which continued to the 1950's when only an occasional working boat used the northern section; the southern section, Lapworth to Stratford, was badly silted. In 1958, following threats of closure, a massive campaign was started to save the canal. The following year it was reprieved, and the National Trust assumed responsibility for restoring and maintaining the southern section. In 1961 restoration work

began, and the canal was re-opened in 1964.

Maximum dimensions
Length: 70'
Beam: 7'
Headroom: 6'
Mileage
KING'S NORTON JUNCTION to
Hockley Heath: 9¾
LAPWORTH junction with Grand Union
Canal: 12½
Preston Bagot: 16¼
Wootton Wawen Basin: 18½
Wilmcote: 22
STRATFORD-ON-AVON junction with
River Avon: 25½
Total 55 locks

The canal is CLOSED from November to February.

Birmingham

7½ miles

The first 5 miles pass through the residential outskirts of Birmingham, but the canal is quiet and bordered with dense but varied vegetation. In conjunction with the northern section of the Worcester & Birmingham Canal, this is a far more interesting route between Lapworth and Birmingham than via the Grand Union Canal. Leaving the Worcester & Birmingham at King's Norton Junction, the Stratford-on-Avon Canal proceeds straight to the well-known King's Norton stop lock which is unusual in having 2 wooden guillotine gates mounted in iron frames balanced by chains and counterweights. The machinery has now seized up, and boats pass under the gates without stopping. East of Brandwood Tunnel there is a bridge with the remains of an old arm just beyond it. A private boatyard lies just around the corner and there is a water point outside a cottage near bridge 5. Access is bad at most of the bridges. Passing over a small aqueduct, the canal reaches a steel lift bridge, which has to be raised and lowered with a windlass. (There are 2 more of these bridges nearer Lapworth). The canal now sheds all traces of the suburbs and maintains a twisting course in a wooded cutting through quiet countryside. Few roads of any significance come near it. At bridge 16 it emerges from a long cutting and is joined by a feeder from the nearby Earlswood Reservoirs. There are no villages along this stretch of canal.

Brandwood Tunnel
352yds long, the tunnel has no towpath. Horse-drawn boats had to be hauled through by means of an iron hand-rail on the side. Lengths of this rail can still be seen.
Earlswood Reservoir
Half a mile south of bridge 16 is this canal-feeding reservoir, surrounded by trees and divided into three lakes: Windmill Pool, Engine Pool and Terry's Pool. There is a sailing club on Terry's Pool, and fishing available to the general public on the other two. The bailiff will supply information about the lakes. (Lapworth 2091).

BOATYARDS & BWB
Ⓑ **Earlswood Marine Services** Lady lane, Earlswood, Warwicks. (2552). Ⓡ Ⓢ Ⓦ Ⓓ . Gas, chandlery, slipway,

moorings. Large trip boats for hire. Licensed club. Base of the Earlswood Yacht Club; visitors welcome. *Open all year.*

BOAT TRIPS

'Cepheus'. Full length motor narrowboat available for party bookings from Earlswood. Bar on board, and carries a maximum of 45 to 50 passengers. All enquiries to Earlswood Marine Services (*see above*). *Open all year.*

PUBS AND RESTAURANTS

Horse Shoe Canalside, at bridge 3. Cold food. *Telephone and petrol nearby.*

Blue Bell Cider house. Canalside, at bridge 19. Good mooring jetty.

Bull's Head ¼ mile S of bridge 17.

Red Lion 500yds S of bridge 16.

Three Maypoles restaurant. Tamworth lane, Shirley (1905). ¼ mile NE of bridge 12. *Closed Sun.*

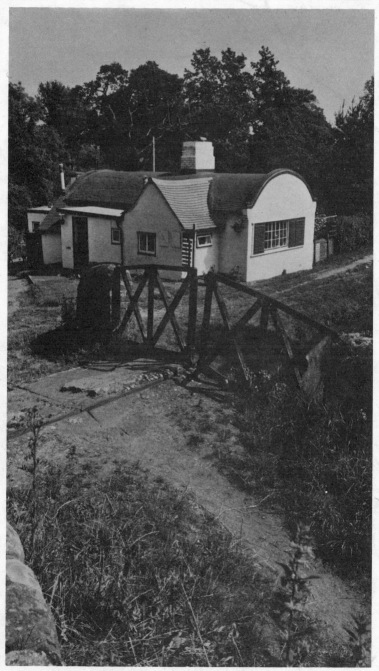

Barrel roof cottage and split bridge, Stratford-on-Avon Canal. *Derek Pratt.*

Stratford upon Avon

18 miles

The canal continues south-eastwards through quiet countryside. At Hockley Heath (bridge 25) is a tiny arm that once served a coal wharf. East of the 2 windlass-operated steel lift bridges that follow, things change dramatically, for the first of the 55 locks down to Stratford is reached. (The top lock is numbered 2, the old stop lock at King's Norton being number 1). After the first 4 locks is a half-mile breathing space, then the Lapworth flight begins in earnest. The short intervening pounds have been enlarged to provide a bigger working reservoir of water, so that one side of each lock is virtually an isthmus. The locks have double bottom gates and are not heavy going. They are interspersed with old cast-iron split bridges. These bridges are built in two halves, separated by a 1-inch gap so that the towing line between a horse and a boat could be dropped through the gap without having to disconnect the horse. Below lock 19 is Kingswood Junction: boats heading for Stratford should keep right here. A short branch to the left through lock 20 leads under the railway line to the Grand Union Canal. (See p.46 of this book.) The Stratford Canal continues south, locking steadily downward. The locks have single gates and very small paddles, so they are slow to fill and empty. The whole southern section is beautifully maintained, quiet and secluded right through to Stratford. Lock 38 at Preston Bagot introduces 2 long pounds, and beyond bridge 53 the canal widens into a basin with a boatyard and pub. At Wilmcote is a private wharf (just S of bridge 59). Boatmen must ask the wharf manager for permission to moor. South of Wilmcote the 11-lock Wilmcote flight begins. At bridge 65 there is a winding hole, petrol station and telephone box. The canal now drops steeply to the splendid basin beside the Shakespeare Memorial Theatre.

Navigational Note
The southern section of the Stratford-on-Avon Canal - i.e. from Lapworth to Stratford- belongs to the National Trust, not the BWB. The Trust has owned the canal since it was restored from dereliction and reopened in 1964. A special licence to navigate the canal must be obtained from the Trust's representative in the Canal Office by lock 21; a map and a very detailed guide book may also be bought here. Facilities for boats are also available.

Lapworth
Warwicks. All services. Both the Stratford-on-Avon and the Grand Union Canals pass through the town. Together with the short spur that connects them, they are one of the most interesting aspects of Lapworth. The 15thC church which lies 1½m W of the junction contains an interesting monument by Eric Gill, 1928.
Packwood House
NT Property. Lapworth (2024). ½m N of B4439 road bridge. 16thC timber-framed house containing collections of tapestry, needlework and furniture. The yew garden is clipped to represent the Sermon on the Mount. *Open Apr-Sep daily except Fri. Oct-Mar closed Tue, Fri.*
Hockley Heath
Warwicks. PO, tel, garage. Convenient for provisions.
Preston Bagot
Warwicks. Some attractive, ancient houses. The church of All Saints has a Norman nave and other Norman details, with Victorian additions.
Lowsonford
Warwicks. PO, tel, stores (all just W of lock 30).
Wilmcote
Warwicks. PO, tel, stores, garage, station. Small, attractive village containing Mary Arden's cottage. The school and vicarage are by Butterfield, c1845. Old-fashioned railway station E of the canal.

Mary Arden's Cottage Wilmcote. The 15thC timbered farmhouse was the home of Shakespeare's mother. Owned by the Shakespeare Birthplace Trust, it contains a museum. *Open daily.*

Edstone (or Bearley) Aqueduct 200yds long, consists of a narrow cast iron trough carried on brick piers. As with the other two, much smaller, aqueducts on this canal, the towpath runs along the level of the bottom of the tank.

Wootten Wawen *Warwicks. PO, tel, stores, garage, station.* Designated a Conservation Area. Plenty of timbered houses. The chief glory is the church of St. Peter which dates from Saxon times. The sanctuary in the centre of the 11thC church remains intact. The nave is conspicuously Norman and the chancel has a superb 14thC east window. The Lady Chapel is like a barn, often sheltering birds.

Wootton Wawen Basin This wide, embanked basin was built when construction of the canal was halted temporarily. The hire cruiser base was awarded a Civic Trust commendation for its design in 1972. The aqueduct that carries the canal over the A34 was opened in 1813. Just down the hill from the aqueduct is a fine late 18thC brick watermill in good repair.

Stratford-upon-Avon *Warwicks. Pop 19,000. EC Thur. MD Wed. All services.* Tourism has been established in Stratford since 1789 when the first big celebrations in William Shakespeare's honour were held. These are still held annually on St. George's Day-23rd April, which is believed to be Shakespeare's birthday. An annual Mop Fair on 12th October is a reminder that Stratford was well established as a market town long before Shakespeare's time. The town manages to retain its ancient charm despite the constant flow of visitors.

Shakespeare Birthplace Trust Founded in 1847 to look after the 5 buildings most closely associated with Shakespeare. Four of these are listed below, the other is Mary Arden's cottage.

Shakespeare's Birthplace Henley st. Early 16thC half-timbered building containing books, manuscripts and exhibits associated with Shakespeare and rooms furnished in period style. Next door is the Shakespeare Centre. *Open daily.*

Hall's Croft Old Town. Tudor house complete with period furniture–the home of Shakespeare's daughter Susanna. *Closed Sun Nov-Mar.*

New Place Chapel st. The foundations of Shakespeare's last home set in a replica of an Elizabethan garden. *Closed Sun Nov-Mar.*

Anne Hathaway's Cottage Shottery. 1m W of Stratford. This fine thatched farmhouse dates from the 15thC and was once the home of Anne Hathaway before she married William Shakespeare. The cottage was damaged by fire in 1969, but has since been completely restored. *Open daily.*

Holy Trinity Church Overlooks the newly restored lock on the River Avon. Mainly 15thC but the spire was rebuilt in 1763. Interesting misericords and fine monuments. Shakespeare is buried in the chancel. His tomb bears a curse against anyone who disturbs it.

Shakespeare Memorial Theatre (box office 2271). Home of the Royal Shakespeare Company, who produce Shakespeare's plays *from Apr to Dec every year.*

Clopton Bridge A fine stone bridge over the Avon, originally built around 1480-90. The brick bridge nearby was built in 1823 to carry a horse-drawn tramway connecting Stratford with Shipston-on-Stour. It is now a footbridge.

Information Centre Judith Shakespeare's House, 1 High st, Stratford-on-Avon (3127). Shakespeare's younger daughter lived in this former tavern.

BOATYARD & BWB

Ⓑ **Swallow Cruisers** Wharf lane, Hockley Heath, Warwicks. (Lapworth 3442). Beside bridge 27. Slipway, gas, boat & engine repairs, mooring, chandlery, toilets.

National Trust Canal Depot Lapworth Junction (2024). Ⓡ Ⓢ Ⓦ Ⓓ Canal maps and guides. This is the Canal Manager's office and the main telephone number for all enquiries about the southern section of the Stratford-on-Avon Canal. *Closed Nov-Mar.*

Ⓑ **Anglo Welsh Narrow Boats** The Wharf, Wootton Wawen, Solihull, Warwicks. (Henley-in-Arden 3427). Ⓦ Ⓓ Pump-out *(Mon-Fri)*. Boat hire, gas, boat & engine repairs, mooring, toilets. *Closed Sun.*

Ⓑ **Western Cruisers** Western rd, Stratford-on-Avon, Warwicks. (69636). Ⓡ Ⓢ Ⓦ Ⓓ Pump-out *(Mar-Oct)*. Boat hire, gas, boat & engine repairs, mooring, chandlery, toilets, showers, bread & milk.

Ⓑ **Stratford-upon-Avon Marine** Clopton Bridge, Stratford-on-Avon, Warwicks. (69669/69773) Ⓡ Ⓢ Ⓦ Ⓓ Pump-out. Gas, chandlery, boat hire, boat building & repairs, mooring, toilets, showers, restaurant. *Closed Sat afternoon and Sun in winter.*

PUBS AND RESTAURANTS

🍺 **Navigation** Lapworth. Canalside, on Grand Union Canal at bridge 65.

🍺 **Boot Inn** Lapworth, near lock 14.

🍺 **Wharf Inn** Hockley Heath. Canalside, at bridge 25. Food. Garden.

🍺 **Old Crab Mill** Preston Bagot, 350yds W of the new road bridge. (Claverdon 2857). *Telephone outside.*

✗ **Mill Cottage Tea Room** Preston Bagot, 300yds W of the new bridge. Light lunches, teas, etc. Home-made cakes. *Daily except Mon.* (Claverdon 2778).

🍺✗ **Fleur de Lys** Lowsonford. By the canal north of lock 31. Garden. (Lapworth 2431). Food.

🍺 **Ye Olde New Inn** Turner's Green. Canalside, on the Grand Union Canal. (½ mile SE of Stratford Canal Bridge 39, beyond the railway).

🍺✗ **Mason's Arms** Wilmcote. Snacks and hot meals *daily except Sun lunch and Mon dinner.* (Curry a speciality). (Stratford-on-Avon 2166).

🍺✗ **Olde Bull's Head** Wootton Wawen. ½ mile W of the aqueduct. Full restaurant meals daily. (Henley-in-Arden 2511).

🍺✗ **Navigation** Wootton Wawen, at the basin. Meals at or near the bar *daily (except Tue)* during licensed hours. Omelettes, steaks, snacks etc. (Henley-in-Arden 2676). There are endless pubs, hotels and restaurants in Stratford, but none actually on the canal.

✗❢ **Marianne** 3 Greenhill st, Stratford-on-Avon (3563). French restaurant near the station. *(Closed Sun).* Booking essential.

✗❢ **Piper at the Gates of Dawn** Stratford Marine, Stratford-on-Avon (69821). Floating restaurant, departs daily for lunch, dinner.

Trent & Mersey Canal

This early canal was originally conceived as a roundabout link between the ports of Liverpool and Hull, passing through the important 'potteries' area. One of its prime movers was Josiah Wedgewood, who together with Thomas Bentley, Erasmus Darwin and other influential friends promoted its building. Its Act was passed by Parliament in 1766; the ageing James Brindley was appointed engineer, and in 1777 it opened, the 2900 yard tunnel through Harecastle Hill attracting much interest. The route became a great success carrying raw materials to the potteries, distributing finished products, stimulating industry and providing jobs. It soon earned its other name 'The Grand Trunk Canal', as no fewer than 9 other canals or major branches joined it. During the 1820's the slowly sinking Harecastle Tunnel was causing delays. Thomas Telford was called in and he recommended building a new tunnel beside the old. This was completed by 1827, and had a much needed towpath. The canal continued to flourish as a major trade route until the Great War, but today carries virtually no commercial traffic, this having been replaced by pleasure craft.

Maximum dimensions

Derwent Mouth to Burton upon Trent
Length: 72'
Beam: 13' 6"
Headroom: 7'
Burton upon Trent to Great Haywood
Length: 72'
Beam: 7'
Headroom: 6' 3"
Great Haywood to Middlewich
Length: 72'
Beam: 7'
Headroom: 5' 9"

Mileage

DERWENT MOUTH to
Horninglow Wharf: $16\frac{1}{2}$
FRADLEY JUNCTION: $26\frac{1}{4}$
GREAT HAYWOOD JUNCTION: 39
Stone: $48\frac{1}{4}$
(Derwent Mouth to Preston Brook: $93\frac{1}{2}$)

$11\frac{1}{4}$ miles

The Trent & Mersey starts at the junctions of the Rivers Trent and Derwent at Derwent Mouth. Heading west the first lock is soon reached this and all the locks to Stenson Lock are 13ft 6ins wide, thereafter they are narrow to Middlewich. Craft with a beam of 13ft 6ins can proceed as far as Dallow Lane Lock, Burton. After the lock is the 'canal village' of Shardlow, one of the most interesting on the whole inland waterways network. (It is also possible to visit the village by river, as the Trent is navigable to here.) Beyond it the valley is wide and flat and the river can be seen to the S, with the towers of Castle Donnington Power Station in the distance. At Weston upon Trent the isolated church with its Victorian Rectory overlooks the valley from a hilltop. To the W of bridge 10 is a farming settlement run entirely by expatriate Ukrainians it can be a shock for the unsuspecting to hear groups of men speaking *Russian* in these parts. The navigation now enters a delightful stretch of thick woods as it approaches the deep Swarkestone Lock. Just above the lock the old Derby Canal used to head off NE it is now disused and dewatered. The countryside is green and pleasant with only the occasional train disturbing the peace. The settlement of Stenson is becoming a popular mooring place the lock here is wide and has a massive 12ft 4ins fall. A new basin has been developed just above the lock.

Shardlow
Derbs. PO, tel, stores, garage. Few canal travellers will want to pass through Shardlow without stopping. It is a magnificent example of a small canal port in a prime state of preservation. Everywhere there are living examples of large-scale canal architecture, as well as old-established necessities like canal pubs and a boat-building yard. By the lock is the biggest and best of these buildings—the 18thC Trent Mill, which has a large central arch for boats to enter and unload, now restored and converted into a marina. Another fine structure is the old warehouse next to the Malt Shovel. This pub has an old plate on an outside wall, showing the date 1799. Opposite, with the tall chimney, is a

maltings where malt is still extracted from
barley, giving at times a marvellous smell.
To the north of the village is an 18thC
stone-fronted hall.

Aston upon Trent
Derbs. PO, tel, stores, petrol. A pleasant
village, nearly a mile from the canal. The
stone church dates from the 12thC and
has good Victorian stained glass.

Weston upon Trent
Derbs. PO, tel, stores. A scattered village
with its church splendidly sited on top of
a hill. Its sturdy tower is crowned by a
short 14thC spire.

Swarkestone
Derbs. PO, tel, stores. Its main feature is
the 5-arched 18thC stone bridge over the
Trent, which extends on stone arches
across the rivers flood plain to the village
of Stanton by Bridge.

Barrow upon Trent
Derbs. PO, tel, stores. A small quiet
village—there is no pub.

BOATYARDS & BWB

Ⓑ **Dobson's Boatyard** The Wharf,
Shardlow. Derbs. (Derby 792271). On the
canal. Ⓡ Ⓢ Ⓦ Ⓓ Pump-out. Boat hire,
slipway, gas, boat building & repair,
mooring, chandlery, toilets, winter storage.
40 seat trip boat 'Aquarius' for charter.

Ⓑ **Plus Pleasure Marina** London rd,
Shardlow (Derby 792844). In the newly
restored Trent corn Mill, just below
Shardlow Lock. Ⓡ Ⓢ Ⓦ Ⓓ Pump-out.
Hire fleet, slipway, gas, chandlery, toilets,
showers, café, shop, exhibition. Trip boat for
charter.

Ⓑ **Clayton Line Stenson Marina**
Stenson, Derby (Repton 3113). Ⓡ Ⓢ Ⓦ Ⓓ
Pump-out. Hire fleet, gas, slipway, mooring,
repairs, groceries, toilets, winter storage,
trip boat. *Closed in winter.*

PUBS

🍺 **Malt Shovel** Shardlow. A popular canal
pub near bridge 2.

🍺 **New Inn** Shardlow, next to the Malt
Shovel.

✕❢ **Lady in Grey** Shardlow (331). Good
restaurant on the canal opposite Dobson's
boatyard.

🍺 **Malt Shovel** Aston.

🍺 **White Hart** Aston.

🍺 **Plough** Weston upon Trent.

🍺 **Crew & Harpur** Swarkestone, by the
river bridge.

Burton upon Trent

15 miles (to Fradley)

The canal continues SW accompanied
closely by the railway, past Findern and
on to Willington, beyond which the dual
carriageway of the A38 closes in to escort
the navigation almost to Alrewas. The
proliferation of petrol stations and the
sprinkling of transport cafés are convenient,
but in no way compensate for the noise
and loss of privacy the road brings.
Approaching Burton the canal passes over
the River Dove on a 9-arched stone
aqueduct, then skirts the NW of the town.
The journey through Burton is pleasant,
punctuated by Dallow Lane Lock, the first of
the narrow locks, then by Horninglow
Wharf where there are often narrow boats
moored. You should be able to detect
cheering brewing smells—for some the
Burton air is the sweetest in the country.
Shobnall Basin (that once served Marston's
Brewery and is now a marina) is left
behind as the canal enters more open country
towards Branston, with the A38 first
crossing, then never far away. The pub at
Branston Bridge is a highly recommended
place in which to sample some of the best of
Burton's produce, before continuing towards
Barton Turn, with its lock and pub, then on
through the delightful watermeadows to
Wychnor. Above bridge 45 the River Trent
joins the canal for a short distance there
is a weir to the SE which can be tricky
Navigators heading *towards Alrewas*
should keep well *to the right*, those
heading *towards Wychnor Lock* should
keep well *to the left*. After the pretty village of
Alrewas the canal passes through flat
countryside to Fradley Junction, where the
Coventry Canal branches SE (see p38)

Findern
Derbs. PO, tel, stores. A small quiet village
where Jedekiah Strutt, the inventor of the
ribbed stocking frame, once served an
apprenticeship. Fine village green, rescued
from extinction by the local W.I.

Willington
Derbs. PO, tel, stores. Busy little village
bisected by the railway embankment.

Repton
One of the oldest towns in England.
Once capital of Mercia, there is much of
historical interest. The crypt below St

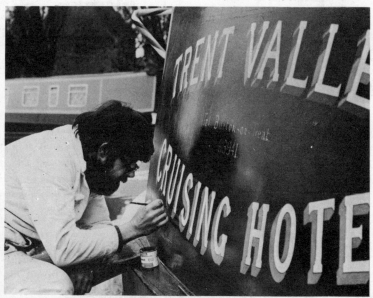

At work, Horninglow Basin, Burton-on-Trent. *Derek Pratt.*

Wystans church was built in the 10thC.
Repton public school dates from 1551.

Egginton
Derbs. PO, tel, stores. A quiet village.
The church has a pleasing irregularity.

Burton upon Trent
*Staffs. Pop 51,000. EC Wed. MD Thur/
Sat. All services.* Brewing is thought to
have been started here by monks in the
13thC. They discovered that the high
gypsum content in the water made for
fine ale. The first brewery was established
in 1708—at one time there were 20 but
alas now only a handful remain. Perhaps
the most widely known of Burton's products
is I.P.A., India Pale Ale. Originally intended
for export, it was released on the home
market by underwriters after being salvaged
when a boat carrying a cargo to India
sank. The street pattern of the town is
influenced by the railway sidings, which
branch through the town at street level—
most are no longer used. As well as many
pubs, there is a Museum and Art Gallery
in Guild street to visit; access to the town
is best from Horninglow Wharf, Dallow
Lane Lock and Shobnall Marina.

The Bass Museum Horninglow st. ¾ mile
from Horninglow Basin. Brewing during the
late 19thC. *Open 10.30–16.30 Mon–Fri,
11.00–17.00 Sat, Sun, Bank hols.*

Branston
Staffs. PO, tel, stores; garage, fish & chips.
Perhaps boaters should venture no
further than the pub by the bridge.

Barton-under-Needwood
Staffs. PO, tel, stores. Long main street
with many attractive pubs. Battlemented
church built in the 16thC. The former
royal forest of Needwood is to the N.
Access was once possible only by turning
off the Roman Ryknild street·at 'Barton
Turn'.

Alrewas
Staffs. PO, tel, stores garage. Once
famous for basket weaving. The canal
ambles through this attractive village,
which has some fine timbered cottages.
There is an old flour mill, still working,
on the River Trent.

Fradley Junction
A fine canal junction, with lots of moored
boats, a pub, a boatyard and a BWB
yard. The Coventry joins the T & M here.

BOATYARDS & BWB

Ⓑ **Jannel Cruisers** Shobnall Marina,
Shobnall rd, Burton on Trent (42718).
In Shobnall Basin. Ⓡ Ⓢ Ⓦ Ⓓ Pump-out.
Hire fleet, gas, dry dock, toilets.
Ⓑ **BWB Fradley Yard** Burton upon Trent
(790236). Ⓡ Ⓢ Ⓦ
Ⓑ **Swan Line Cruisers** Fradley Junction,
Alrewas, Burton upon Trent, Staffs. (Burton
upon Trent 790332). Ⓦ Ⓓ Pump-out
(*not weekends*). Hire cruisers. Gas, chandlery
Drydock, moorings. Boat building, sales
and repairs, inboard engine sales and
repairs. Groceries. *Closed winter weekends.*

PUBS

🍺 **Greyhound** Findern. Canalside, at
bridge 21. Large garden for children, and
outside bar (sometimes). Many moored
boats here.
🍺 **Green Man** Willington.
🍺 **Rising Sun** Willington.
🍺 **Green Dragon** Willington.
All 3 pubs at Willington are near bridge 23.
🍺 **Every Arms,** On A38 west of bridge
25 (but access only from bridge 26 to
avoid crossing private land). Cold snacks.
🍺 **Navigation** near Horninglow Wharf
Pubs in Burton are not scarce.
🍺 **Bridge** Canalside, at Branston Bridge
(34). Garden; excellent beer from the cask.
Bar snacks all year, pub lunches *Nov–Feb.*
🍺 **Vine** Barton Turn, just opposite Barton
Lock.
🍺✕ **Bell** Barton-under-Needwood
(2249). Restaurant (*closed Sun evenings
and all day Mon*).
🍺 **Three Horseshoes** Barton-under-
Needwood. Food.
🍺 **Crown** Alrewas, near bridge 46.
🍺✕ **Navigation** Alrewas, near Bagnall
Lock. Bar snacks, no meals *Mon evenings.*
🍺 **Swan** Fradley Junction. Canalside;
focus of the junction. Snacks.

Great Haywood

16½ miles

Approaching Rugeley, the towers and
chimneys of the power station come into
view and eventually dominate the scene.
Past here there is an attractive and
interesting area. Cannock Chase is visible
to the S, Shugborough Hall is to the W
and the Staffordshire and Worcestershire
Canal (see p 65) joins at Great Haywood
Junction. Beyond here the Trent Valley
becomes more open with woods and quiet
meadows. There are few locks before
Stone which is a good place to moor
with shops and a pub near the canal.

Rugeley
Staffs. Pop 18,000. PO, tel, stores, garage.
An unexciting place dominated by the
power station.

Great Haywood
Staffs. PO, tel, stores. Centre of the
Great Haywood and Shugborough Conservation Area. The village is linked to
Shugborough Park by the very old packhorse bridge. Haywood Lock is beautifully
situated near this bridge and the decorative
railway bridge that leads into Trent lane,
which consists of symmetrical and
handsome terraced cottages.

Shugborough Hall
NT Property. A splendid mansion dating
from 1693 and containing magnificent
rooms and many treasures.

Museum of Staffordshire Life In the
stables of the Hall. An excellent establish-
ment—exhibits include a laundry, the gun
room and the old estate brew house.
There is an industrial annexe nearby
containing some steam locomotives.

Shugborough Park Contains some remarkable stone monuments created by James
'Athenian' Stewart in 1762. *Home, grounds
and museum closed Mon in summer; Sat,
Mon and some Suns in winter.* Enquiries
to Little Haywood 388.

Ingestre Hall
Neo-Gothic style Hall used as a residential
arts centre. *Open first Sat in July.*

Sandon
Staffs. Tel. A small estate village with
a 13-15thC church, clustered near the
gates of:

Burston
Staffs. Tel. A very quiet hamlet around
a pond.

Stone
*Staffs. Pop 10,000. EC Wed. MD Tue,
Thur. All services.* A busy and pleasant
town with excellent shops and facilities
for navigators. St Michael's church (1758)
in Lichfield rd is a handsome building.

BOATYARDS & BWB

Ⓑ **Midland Luxury Cruisers** Hoo Mill
Lock, Great Haywood, Stafford. (Little
Haywood 384). Ⓟ Gas. Slipway,
moorings, winter storage. Inboard engine
repairs. Runabouts etc. for hire daily or
hourly.

Ⓑ **Anglo.Welsh Narrowboats** The Canal
Wharf, Mill Lane, Great Haywood. Staffs.
(Little Haywood 711). Ⓡ Ⓢ Ⓦ Ⓓ Pump-
out (*Mon–Fri*). Boat hire, boat & engine
repairs, mooring, toilets.

Ⓑ **Midland Luxury Cruisers** Newcastle
rd, Stone, Staffs. (2688) Ⓡ Ⓢ Ⓦ Ⓟ Hire
cruisers. Gas, chandlery. Slipway, moorings,
winter storage. Boat building, sales &
repairing. Inboard & outboard engine sales
& repairs. Lavatories.

Ⓑ **Canal Cruising Co.** Stone, Staffs.
(813982) Ⓡ Ⓓ Pump-out. Boat hire,
slipway, gas, dry dock, boat building &
repairs, toilets.

PUBS

Ⓟ **Wolseley Arms** near bridge 70.
Ⓟ **Lamb & Flag** Little Haywood.
Ⓟ **Fox & Hounds** Great Haywood.
Ⓟ✕ **Coach & Horses** near bridge 77.
Ⓟ **Saracen's Head** Weston, by bridge 80.
Ⓟ **Dog & Doublet** Sandon. Food.
Closed Sun.
Ⓟ **Greyhound** Burston. Food.
Ⓟ **Star** Canalside, at Stone bottom lock.
Ⓟ✕ **The Scotch Brook.** Stone, 100
yds from bridge 94.

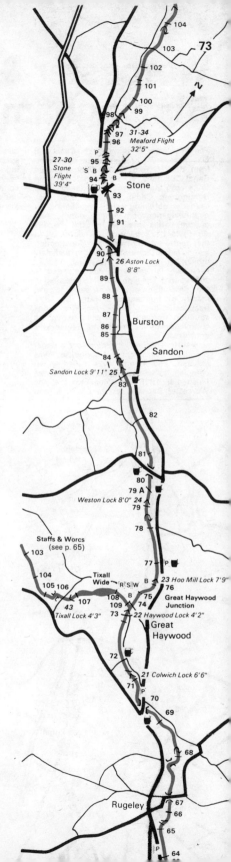

73

27-30
Stone
Flight
39'4"

31-34
Meaford Flight
32'5"

Stone

26 Aston Lock
8'8"

Burston

Sandon

Sandon Lock 9'11" 25

Weston Lock 8'0" 24

Staffs & Worcs
(see p. 65)

Tixall
Wide

23 Hoo Mill Lock 7'9"

Great Haywood
Junction

Tixall Lock 4'3"

22 Haywood Lock 4'2"

Great
Haywood

21 Colwich Lock 6'6"

Rugeley

Worcester & Birmingham

The Worcester & Birmingham Canal Bill was passed in 1791, despite opposition from the Staffordshire & Worcestershire Canal Company, who saw trade on their route to the Severn threatened. The Birmingham Canal Company also succeeded in obtaining a clause preventing the new navigation from coming within 7 feet of theirs–this resulted in the famous Worcester Bar separating the two canals in the centre of Birmingham. Construction started at the Birmingham end; immediately difficulties arose with the water supply–eventually ten reservoirs were planned or constructed. The high cost of this resulted in the construction of a narrow canal, to save money on building and water. By 1817 boats could get to Tardebigge Wharf; construction stopped at this point while the completion of the line to the Severn was considered.

A system of boat lifts down to Worcester proposed by John Woodhouse was rejected, and Rennie was called in to complete the work using 58 locks. This was finished in 1815–the same year that the Worcester Bar was replaced with a stop lock. The canal prospered for a while, then succumbed to railway competition. Carrying continued until about 1964, mainly between two Cadbury factories. But now commercial traffic has been replaced with cruisers securing the future of this outstanding canal.

Maximum dimensions
Length: 71'6"
Beam: 7'
Headroom: 6'
Mileage
WORCESTER, Diglis Basin to
Tibberton: 5¾
Dunhampstead: 7½
Hanbury Wharf: 9¼
Stoke Wharf: 12¾
Tardebigge top lock: 15½
Bittell Reservoirs: 20½
KING'S NORTON JUNCTION: 24½
BIRMINGHAM Worcester Bar Basin: 30
Total 58 locks

7½ miles

The Worcester & Birmingham Canal leaves the Severn climbing through two wide (18ft) locks into Diglis Basin (see map p75), to the south of Worcester. It passes through the town at first hemmed in by buildings, then through waste ground–regrettably not yet acknowledged by the town as a possible amenity. The first of the narrow locks are very deep, a typical feature of this navigation. Tollandine Lock, with its pretty cottage and garden marks the start of open country, with Worcester left well behind and the route becoming increasingly rural. Only the motorway crossing over at Tibberton and the occasional train disturbs the peace. The tunnel at Dunhampstead has a handrail still in place which would pull a boat through while the horse walked over the hill.

Worcester
See page 57 for details.
Diglis Basin
This is a fascinating terminus at the junction of the River Severn and the Worcester & Birmingham Canal. It consists of basins, boatyards, old warehouses and a drydock. Commercial craft have been entirely replaced by a mixture of pleasure boats designed for narrow canals, rivers and the sea. There are 2 boatyards, a chandlery, and the usual BWB facilities. Permission to use the drydock should be sought from the BWB basin attendant, whose house is at the top of the 2 locks down into the river: *telephone Worcester 354323.* The locks will take boats up to 72ft by 18ft 6in, although obviously only narrow boats can proceed along the canal beyond the first lock. The locks (which can be operated only by the basin attendant, *between 8.00 and 19.00*) incorporate a side pond to save water; and near the second lock is a small pump house that raises water from the river to maintain the level in the basin.
Dunhampstead
Worcs. PO, tel, stores (the PO is a few hundred yards NW of bridge 30). Five buildings and a signal box. Life centres on the canal and the pub as trains roar by.
Tibberton
Worcs. PO, tel, stores (all to the south of the pubs). A small but expanding canalside village, of little interest. There is a fine old rectory by the Victorian church.

BOATYARDS & BWB

Ⓑ **Tolladine Boat Services** Diglis Basin, Worcester (352142). Boat builders, repairers and engineers. 10 ton gantry crane and moorings (some undercover).

Ⓑ **Diglis Boat Co** Wharf Cottage, Diglis Basin (Worcester 354039). Ⓡ Ⓢ Ⓦ Dry dock, boat building & repairs, toilets. Boat brokerage a speciality.

Ⓑ **Sovereign Marine** Worcester (54474). By bridge no. 9. Central Booking Office, Lowesmoor Wharf. (27022). Ⓡ Ⓢ Ⓦ Ⓓ Pump-out (*not Sat*). Gas, boat building, boat and engine repairs, mooring, toilets, winter storage, boat hire.

Ⓑ **Brook Line** Dunhampstead Wharf,

Oddingly (Droitwich 3889). Ⓡ Ⓢ Ⓦ Ⓓ Pump-out. Boat hire, gas, boat building & repair, chandlery, toilets, winter storage. Trip boat and day boats

PUBS

🍺 **Anchor** Diglis, on the road just outside the basin grounds.

🍺 **Bricklayers Arms** Worcester near Blockhouse Lock.

🍺 **Bridge** Worcester canalside at bridge 9.

🍺 **Cavalier Tavern** Worcester canalside at bridge 11.

🍺 **God Speed the Plough** Tibberton.

🍺 **Bridge** Tibberton. Garden.

🍺 **Fir Tree** Dunhampstead. Popular pub with a garden.

DIGLIS BASIN

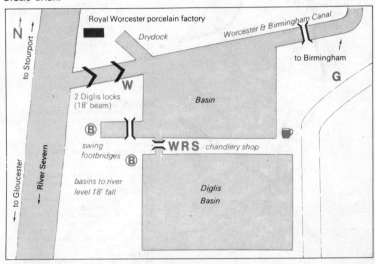

Royal Worcester porcelain factory

N ↑ to Stourport

Drydock

Worcester & Birmingham Canal

to Birmingham

G

W

2 Diglis locks (18' beam)

Basin

Ⓑ

swing footbridges

Ⓑ

WRS *chandler shop*

basins to river level 18' fall

River Severn

to Gloucester

Diglis Basin

The Worcester & Birmingham Canal's secluded course through Edgbaston.

Tardebigge

17 miles

While on the longest pound between Worcester and Tardebigge Top Lock, with the hills still away to the east, the navigator should rest and contemplate the task ahead. After the busy area of Hanbury Wharf, where the now unnavigable Droitwich Canal joins, Astwood Locks appear, set in rural pastureland. Passing through Stoke Works the hills begin to close in, and immediately after the six locks of the Stoke flight the *thirty* Tardebigge Locks begin. Progress is reduced to a crawl; but attractive countryside, well-preserved cottages and gardens, and the traditional locks with wooden balance beams provide adequate compensation. The large paddles speed up the locking, and eventually you will have climbed 217 feet. Tardebigge Top Lock is notable for its 14ft fall, one of the deepest narrow locks in the country. You can now cool off in the tunnel, secure in the knowledge of no more locks before Gas Street. Continuing northward through tranquil countryside the canal passes through Shortwood Tunnel, then the long King's Norton Tunnel, from which you emerge into Warwickshire and the start of the Black Country.

Hanbury Wharf
A short arm leads to the original wharf, now overshadowed by a busy modern boatyard.
Hanbury Hall
Footpath SE from lock 17. Wren-style red brick house, 1701. *Open Wed & Sat afternoons in summer.*
Stoke Works
Built in 1828 to pump brine (salt) from underground for industrial use.
Stoke Wharf
A pretty canal settlement with a lock, a wharf, a warehouse and a pub.
Avoncroft Museum of Buildings
Stoke Prior (Bromsgrove 31363). Buildings from an Iron age hut to a local chain and nail works on display. *Open Tue–Sun mid Mar–mid Oct.*
Tardebigge
Worcs. Stores. A small farming village. 18thC church with a delicate spire.
Tardebigge and Shortwood Tunnels
568 and 608yds respectively, the second being extremely wet. Neither has a towpath.
Alvechurch
Worcs, PO, tel, stores. A pleasant little town with some half timbered houses. Butterfield rebuilt the Norman church in 1861.
Bittel Reservoirs
The upper is a canal feeder, the lower was built to compensate mill owners for loss of water with the building of the canal.
King's Norton Tunnel
Otherwise known as Wast or West Hill Tunnel. 2726yds, one of the longest in the country. A steam and later diesel powered tug used to operate in the horse-drawn days. Grandiose bridges span the cuttings at either end.
King's Norton
West Midlands. PO, tel, stores, garage. Still surviving as a village, in spite of Brums suburban tentacles all around. A village green, a mainly 14thC church with a soaring spire and a grammar school, probably founded by Edward III in 1344 and now an ancient monument.

BOATYARDS & BWB
Ⓑ **Ladyline** Hanbury rd, Droitwich, Worcs (3002). Ⓡ Ⓢ Ⓦ Boat sales, gas, chandlery, toilets, showers.
Ⓑ **BWB Tardebigge Yard** Tardebigge Top Lock. (Bromsgrove 72572) Ⓡ Ⓢ Ⓦ Drydock available, also permanent moorings.
Ⓑ **Black Prince Narrow Boats** Stoke Wharf, Nr Bromsgrove, Worcs. (70300). Ⓡ Ⓢ Ⓦ Ⓓ Pump-out. Boat hire, gas, mooring, chandlery, toilets, provisions.
Ⓑ **Alvechurch Boat Centre** Scarfield Wharf, Alvechurch, Birmingham. (021 445 2909). At bridge 60 Ⓡ Ⓢ Ⓦ Ⓟ Ⓓ Pump-out. Narrow boat hire. Marine

Map labels

76

Edgbaston

Stratford-on-Avon Canal (see p. 66)

Bournville Garden Factory

77
75
74
73
72
71
70

Kings Norton Junction

King's Norton

Kings Norton Tunnel

69
68
67
66
65
64
63
62
61
60
59

B
P

Alvechurch

Shortwood Tunnel

58
57

Tardebigge Tunnel

BWB Tardebigge Yard Ⓡ Ⓢ Ⓦ
Tardebigge Top Lock **58**

Tardebigge

29-58
Tardebigge Locks
217'0"

51

29
48
28
Ⓦ

23-28
Stoke Locks
42'0"

23

Stoke Wharf 44

43

42

Stoke Works

41

22

17-22
Astwood Locks
42'0"

40

17

38
37
36

35 Hanbury Wharf

34 33

engineering of all kinds; boat fitting out, repairs and sales. Engine installation and repairs, gas, chandlery, slipway, permanent moorings, winter storage, toilets. Groceries nearby, over canal bridge.

Ⓡ **Marine Sales & Service** Birmingham rd, Hopwood, near Alvechurch, Birmingham. (021 445 2595)! Ⓡ Ⓦ Ⓟ Ⓓ Small slipway; light boat repairs. Outboard and inboard engine repairs. Boatbuilding and fitting out. Gas, mooring, chandlery, winter storage.

PUBS

🍺 **Eagle & Sun** Hanbury Wharf, canalside.
🍺 **Bowling Green** Near Astwood Locks.
🍺 **Boat & Railway** Stoke Works. Terrace to canal. Good local. Pickled eggs.
🍺 **Navigation** Stoke Wharf.
🍺 **Queens Head** Canalside at bridge 48.
🍺✕ **The Engine House** Tardebigge. By lock 57.
🍺 **Crown** Alvechurch. canalside.
🍺 **Hopwood House** Canalside at bridge 67. Food usually available.
🍺 **Navigation Inn** King's Norton, near bridge 71.

Edgbaston
5½ miles

At King's Norton Junction the Stratford-on-Avon Canal heads off east through the famous guillotine stop lock (see p66) while the Worcs & Birmingham enters a brief, but grim, industrial area. Thankfully this soon ends as the canal passes through the interesting Cadbury's Bournville Works, now joined by the railway which accompanies it almost to Gas Street. Together they head towards Brum through pleasant surroundings and in splendid isolation. The navigation passes Birmingham University and the Botanical Gardens before reaching Edgbaston Tunnel (105yds), after which it turns sharply west to Gas Street Basin, only its last few hundred yards being typically urban. Its terminus is the stop lock, once a physical barrier known as the Worcester Bar. The Birmingham Canal continues on from the stop lock (see p25) to Farmers Bridge Junction. Here the Birmingham & Fazeley heads off NE and a short distance along is Cambrian Wharf, a restored Basin with a canalside walk, two terraces of 18thC cottages and a pub, the 'Long Boat', with many canal relics, one of the bars a converted narrow boat. From here the B & F descends 13 locks to Aston Junction through drab surroundings, frequently covered over by bridges and buildings; indeed almost subterranean. At the junction, the Digbeth Branch drops down

Tardebigge Locks, on the Worcester & Birmingham. *Derek Pratt.*

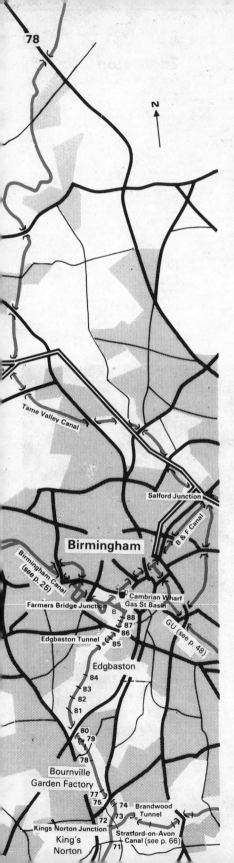

N

Edgbaston (cont)

six locks to the SE and its connection with the Grand Union (see page 48 of this book). The B & F continues on its dull journey down the 11 Aston Locks to Salford Junction. Only near here does it become brighter, with a half-sunken narrowboat making a watergarden for many flowering weeds. The Birmingham & Fazeley Canal, and its route from here to Fazeley, is described on pages 33–34.

Edgbaston
A desirable residential suburb of Birmingham, renowned for cricket. Several places of interest including:
Cannon Hill Park Formal gardens and the home of Birmingham Zoo.
Cannon Hill Museum For children primarily–bird watching, bee keeping, fishing and pets. *Closed Tue.*
Geological Department Museum The University. *Open daily by arrangement 021 472 1301.*
Botanical Gardens Over 100 years old. *Open daily.*
Perrott's Folly This 7 storey tower was built in 1758. Used as an observatory since the late 1800's.
The Dudley Canal
Used to join the W & B at Selly Oak, but now the eastern end is no more, due to the collapse of the claustrophobic 3795yd Lappal Tunnel.
Bournville Garden Factory
Creation of the Cadbury family (the chocolate people). The Bournville estate is an interesting controlled suburban development started in the late 1800's. Selly Manor and Minworth Greaves are two half-timbered houses of the 13thC and 14thC, rebuilt in the 20's and 30's in Bournville. The old canal wharves that used to serve the factory can still be seen.
Salford Junction
The Birmingham & Fazeley, the Saltley Cut and the Tame Valley Canals meet here, overshadowed by 'Spaghetti Junction', the notorious Gravelly Hill interchange on the motorway. Roads and noise fill the sky–but it's interesting.
The Digbeth Branch
Joins the B & F to the Grand Union, six locks below.
Cambrian Wharf
A restored Basin that won a Civic Trust award in 1970. A vision of what could happen elsewhere.
Worcester Bar or Gas Street Basin
An authentic canal settlement in the middle of contemporary Birmingham.

BOATYARDS & BWB
Ⓑ **Canal Shop & Information Centre** 2 Kingston row, Birmingham (021 236 2645). Chandlery. canal publications and wares for sale. leaflets about cruising in general. Ⓡ Ⓢ Ⓦ Pump-out. Moorings and facilities at Cambrian Wharf.

PUBS
🍺 **Country Girl** Selly Oak, near bridge 78. Food at lunchtime.
🍺 **White Horse** Selly Oak, near bridge 80.
🍺 **Duke of Wellington** near the second lock from Salford Junction, on the Birmingham & Fazeley Canal.
🍺 **Long Boat** Cambrian Wharf, Birmingham. Canalside, near the top lock. Large new canal pub, whose 'garden furniture' includes an old canal crane and dock gates. Interior fittings include an original Bolinder engine and butty boat rudders. One of the bars is in a floating narrowboat. Food usually available.
✕🍴 **The Opposite Lock** Gas Street Basin. A canalside pub for motor-racing types. Others (like boaters) may be admitted if they are presentable. Wining, dining and dancing. *Mon-Sat.* Enquiries to 021 643 2573.

BWB Offices

Headquarters

Melbury House, Melbury Terrace, London NW1 6JX (01 262 6711).
General and Official enquiries and correspondence.

Willow Grange, Church road, Watford, Herts. (Watford 26422).
Pleasure craft licences and registration, mooring permits and angling
arrangements.

Birmingham Area Engineer

Reservoir House, Icknield Port road, Birmingham (021 454 7091).
Responsible for maintaining the waterways listed below.

Birmingham Canal Navigations   Maintenance Yard, Icknield Port Road,
  Birmingham (021 454 2240), Sneyd lane, Bloxwich (76851).
Grand Union Canal Hatton, Canal lane, Hatton, Warwicks.
Oxford Hillmorton, Rugby, Warwicks (2393).
Worcester & Birmingham Canal   Canal Office, Tardebigge (Bromsgrove
  72572).
Staffordshire & Worcester Canal   Canal Basin, Stourport-on-
  Severn (2838).
Stourbridge Canal
Stratford upon Avon Canal

Gloucester Area Enginer

Dock Office, Gloucester (25524). Responsible for maintaining the waterways
listed below.

Severn Navigation   Diglis Lock, Worcester (356264).

Northwich Area Engineer

Navigation road, Northwich, Ches. (Northwich 74321). Responsible for
maintaining the waterways listed below.
Staffs and Worcs Canal
Trent & Mersey Canal Fradley Junction, Alrewas, Burton on Trent (790236)

Nottingham Area Engineer

24 Meadow lane, Nottingham. (Nottingham 862411). Responsible for
maintaining the waterways listed below.

Soar Navigation Loughborough Yard, Loughborough (2729).
Trent & Mersey Canal Loughborough Yard (2729).

Canalphone

A BWB service. 24 hr recorded message about stoppages and events on their
waterways. Telephone **01-723 8486** for **North** of Worcester on Worcester &
Birmingham, Napton Junction on the Oxford, Norton Junction on the Grand
Union. Telephone **01-723 8487** for **South** of Autherley Junction on the
Shropshire Union, Fradley Junction on the Trent & Mersey, Trent Junction on
the River Soar.

80

Index